W9-BCA-808

ESSENTIAL CHEMISTRY

ATOMS, MOLECULES, AND COMPOUNDS

ESSENTIAL CHEMISTRY

Atoms, Molecules, and Compounds

Chemical Reactions

Metals

The Periodic Table

States of Matter

ESSENTIAL CHEMISTRY

ATOMS, MOLECULES, AND COMPOUNDS

PHILLIP MANNING

CHELSEA HOUSE
PUBLISHERS
An imprint of Infobase Publishing

ATOMS, MOLECULES, AND COMPOUNDS

Chelsea House
An imprint of Infobase Publishing
132 West 31st Street
New York NY 10001

Library of Congress Cataloging-in-Publication Data
Manning, Phillip, 1936-
  Atoms, molecules, and compounds / Phillip Manning.
      p. cm. — (Essential chemistry)
  Includes bibliographical references and index.
  ISBN-13: 978-0-7910-9534-8 (hardcover)
  ISBN-10: 0-7910-9534-7 (hardcover)
  1. Atoms. 2. Molecules. 3. Matter—Constitution. 4. Chemical reactions. I. Title. II. Series.

QC173.M335 2007
539.7—dc22   2007011403

Chelsea House books are available at special discounts when purchased in bulk quantities for businesses, associations, institutions, or sales promotions. Please call our Special Sales Department in New York at (212) 967-8800 or (800) 322-8755.

You can find Chelsea House on the World Wide Web at http://www.chelseahouse.com

Text design by Erik Lindstrom
Cover design by Ben Peterson

Printed in the United States of America

Bang FOF 10 9 8 7 6 5 4 3 2 1

This book is printed on acid-free paper.

All links and Web addresses were checked and verified to be correct at the time of publication. Because of the dynamic nature of the Web, some addresses and links may have changed since publication and may no longer be valid.

CONTENTS

Meet the Atom

Richard Feynman loved to play the bongos. He also loved solving problems. He figured out the reason for the space shuttle *Challenger's* 1986 explosion by showing that cold weather caused the rubber seals of the booster rocket to fail. Feynman was one of the twentieth century's great theoretical physicists, a Nobel Prize winner who spent much of his career studying **atoms**. He knew as much about atoms as anyone in the world, and this is what he said about them in his book *Six Easy Pieces:*

> If, in some cataclysm, all of scientific knowledge were to be destroyed, and only one sentence passed on to the next generations of creatures, what statement would contain the most information in the fewest words? I believe it is the *atomic hypothesis* (or the atomic *fact,* or whatever you wish to call it) that *all things are made of atoms—little particles that move around in perpetual*

motion, attracting each other when they are a little distance apart, but repelling upon being squeezed into one another.

As usual, Feynman was right. His "little particles" captures an essential fact about atoms. They are tiny—so tiny that a teaspoon of water contains about 500,000,000,000,000,000,000,000 of them. Handling numbers this big is awkward. Try dividing it by 63, for example. To accommodate the very large numbers encountered in counting atoms and the very small ones needed to measure them, chemists use the **scientific notation** system.

Scientific notation uses exponents to express numbers. The number 1,000, for instance, is equal to $10 \times 10 \times 10$, or 10^3. The number of zeros following the 1 in 1,000 is 3, the same as the exponent in scientific notation. Similarly, 10,000, with 4 zeros, would be 10^4, and so on. The same rules apply to numbers that are not even multiples of 10. For example, the number 1,360 is 1.36×10^3. And the number of atoms in a spoonful of water becomes an easy-to-write 5×10^{23}.

Scientific notation is also useful for representing very small numbers. The number 0.1 would be 1/10 or 10^{-1}. The radius of an atom of aluminum is 0.000000000143 meters. Using scientific notation, we could write this distance more compactly as 1.43×10^{-10}. Atoms are, indeed, very "little particles."

An astonishing fact illustrates how small and how numerous atoms are. Pour yourself a glass of water. Now, attach an imaginary tag to each atom. Carry the glass to the ocean and dump it in. Now comes the hard part. Stir the ocean until the tagged atoms are distributed evenly, just as you would add a powdered drink to a glass of water and stir it to get a uniform color. Now dip your glass into the ocean. Would you get any tagged atoms? The answer is: yes! Several million of them, in fact. Surprisingly, there are many more atoms in an ordinary glass of water than there are glasses of water in all the Earth's oceans.

EARLY HISTORY OF THE ATOM

The first person to record his ideas about these "little particles" was the Greek philosopher Democritus, who lived over 2,000 years ago. According to Democritus, whose theory was more philosophical than scientific, all **matter** was made up of tiny particles. Today, these particles are called atoms after the Greek word *atomos,* which means indivisible. Democritus got a lot right in his theory of matter, which survived for centuries. One of the things he got wrong, though, was the types of atoms he said existed. Democritus believed that all atoms contained the same amount of matter, although they could morph from one shape to another. Democritus thought that variations in ordinary substances, such as the difference between sulfur and iron, were due to the shapes the atoms assumed and to the way they clustered together.

Chemists know differently today. Chemically distinguishable atoms are found in 92 naturally occurring forms, from hydrogen to uranium. The man who provided the insight that led to that knowledge was an Englishman named John Dalton (1766–1844). Raised a Quaker, Dalton was a man of simple tastes, unchanging habits, and a brilliant mind. By the age of 12, he was teaching school, a profession he worked at until his death. Dalton's research—which he also pursued until his death—was widely recognized as being crucially important to the advancement of science. Consequently, this modest man became so famous that 40,000 people attended his funeral.

In addition to his research in chemistry and physics, Dalton investigated color blindness, an ailment he suffered from. However, he is best known for his work in the early 1800s in which he noticed that substances always combined in fixed proportions. A fixed weight of oxygen always combines with a fixed weight of hydrogen to produce a predictable amount of water. The Law of Fixed Proportions led Dalton to propose the first scientific theory of the atom:

1. All matter is composed of tiny, indivisible particles called atoms.
2. All atoms of any **element** are identical. That is, all oxygen atoms are alike, as are all atoms of hydrogen.
3. Atoms of different elements are not alike. Oxygen atoms differ from hydrogen atoms in many ways, including weight.
4. **Compounds** are formed by joining the atoms of two or more elements. When forming a compound, the atoms of elements combine in whole-number ratios, such as 1 to 1, 2 to 1, 3 to 2, and so on. Water, with two atoms of hydrogen for every atom of oxygen, would be a compound with a ratio of 2 to 1.

Like Democritus, Dalton got much right. But the concept of atoms as indivisible particles would soon be overthrown.

BUILDING AN ATOM

Science demonstrations were a popular novelty in the 1800s. Lecturers traveled from town to town showing off the latest scientific gadgets. Devices that produced colorful, mysterious effects attracted the biggest crowds. One of the most popular demonstrations featured a glass tube with most of the air pumped out. When an electrical current was applied, lovely colorful patterns appeared in the tube. Violet streamers stretched across empty space from the negatively charged **cathode** to a positively charged electrode called an **anode**. Scientists desperately wanted to know what was happening inside these tubes. Over the years, in experiment after experiment, the evidence gradually accumulated:

- When a solid object was placed between the cathode and anode, a shadow appeared at the end of the tube where the anode was located. This indicated that discharges came from the cathode and traveled in a straight line. Because of this, they were called **cathode rays**, and the tube was dubbed a **cathode ray tube** or CRT (Figure 1.1).

- One clever experimenter placed a tiny paddle wheel in the path of cathode rays. The rays turned the wheel, indicating that they were actually particles.
- Another experiment showed that cathode rays were deflected by a magnetic field. This meant that they were electrically charged particles.

The questions that remained were daunting. How big were these particles and how big was the charge they carried? And, most

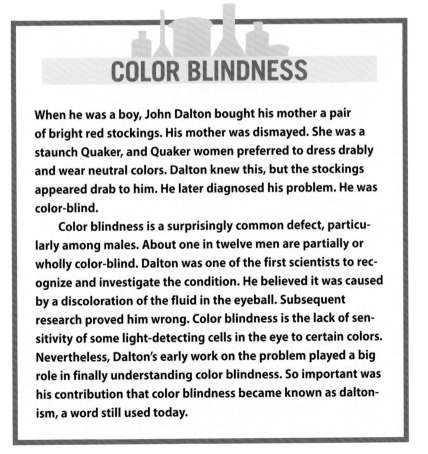

COLOR BLINDNESS

When he was a boy, John Dalton bought his mother a pair of bright red stockings. His mother was dismayed. She was a staunch Quaker, and Quaker women preferred to dress drably and wear neutral colors. Dalton knew this, but the stockings appeared drab to him. He later diagnosed his problem. He was color-blind.

Color blindness is a surprisingly common defect, particularly among males. About one in twelve men are partially or wholly color-blind. Dalton was one of the first scientists to recognize and investigate the condition. He believed it was caused by a discoloration of the fluid in the eyeball. Subsequent research proved him wrong. Color blindness is the lack of sensitivity of some light-detecting cells in the eye to certain colors. Nevertheless, Dalton's early work on the problem played a big role in finally understanding color blindness. So important was his contribution that color blindness became known as daltonism, a word still used today.

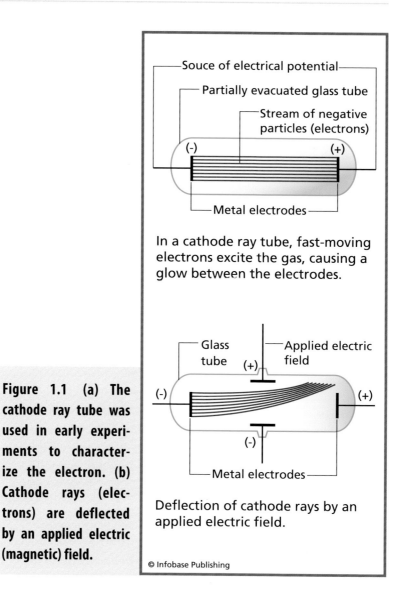

Souce of electrical potential

Partially evacuated glass tube

Stream of negative particles (electrons)

(-)   (+)

Metal electrodes

In a cathode ray tube, fast-moving electrons excite the gas, causing a glow between the electrodes.

Glass tube   Applied electric field

(+)

(-)   (+)

(-)

Metal electrodes

Deflection of cathode rays by an applied electric field.

Figure 1.1 (a) The cathode ray tube was used in early experiments to characterize the electron. (b) Cathode rays (electrons) are deflected by an applied electric (magnetic) field.

© Infobase Publishing

importantly, were they atoms? Joseph John (J.J.) Thomson, the man who would answer these questions, was an established scientist in the late nineteenth century. He held the prestigious position of Cavendish Professor of Experimental Physics at Cambridge University in England. In a series of meticulous experiments, he began to characterize the mysterious rays. First, he showed that cathode rays in an electric field were deflected away from the negatively charged plate. Because opposite charges attract and like charges repel, Thomson concluded that the charge on the rays must be negative. Finally, by carefully measuring how much the negatively charged particles were bent by electric and magnetic fields, Thomson could calculate the ratio of the **mass** of the particle to its charge. To his surprise, the mass-to-charge ratio was one thousandth that of a hydrogen **ion**. (A hydrogen ion is a hydrogen atom that has lost one electron, giving it a positive charge.) Cathode rays either carried a huge charge, or else the particle was much smaller than hydrogen, the smallest atom.

JOSEPH JOHN (J.J.) THOMSON (1856–1940)

J.J. Thomson was born near Manchester, England. He was an outstanding student and attended Trinity College at Cambridge University. He finished second in a grueling, college-wide test in mathematics. Four years after graduating, he was appointed head of the Cavendish research lab at Cambridge.

With Thomson's benevolent support, the men and women at Cavendish did critically important research on the structure of the atom. Seven of them went on to secure the biggest prize in science, the Nobel. Thomson himself won the Nobel Prize for physics in 1906, as well as many other scientific honors. Surprisingly, this outstanding scientist and research director was not a very good experimentalist. "J.J. was very awkward with his fingers," said one of his assistants, "and I found it very necessary not to encourage him to handle the instruments. But he was very helpful in talking over the ways in which he thought things ought to go."[1]

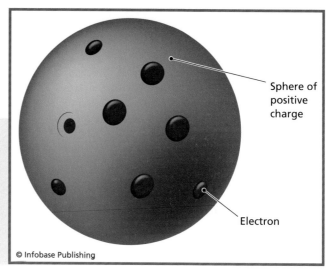

Sphere of
positive
charge

Electron

© Infobase Publishing

Figure 1.2 The plum pudding model of the atom consisted of electrons scattered in a sphere of positive charge.

Work by other scientists showed that cathode ray particles were indeed much smaller than hydrogen. This led Thomson to an astounding conclusion. Cathode rays must be a part of an atom, he announced to the world in 1897. This was big news. All atomic theories before this one, going back to Democritus, held that the atom was indivisible. Now, here was J.J. Thomson saying it was made up of even smaller particles. These particles were soon named **electrons**.

But how could one build an atom out of these tiny negatively charged particles? After all, atoms themselves carried no charge. To offset the negative charge of the electrons, there must be positive charges elsewhere in the atom. Seven years after discovering the electron, Thomson completed his theory of atomic structure. Atoms were, he said, composed of electrons distributed in a soup (or cloud) of positively charged material. The electrons were free to rotate in orbits in the soup, and their negative charges exactly offset the positively charged soup. Thomson's atom was usually pictured as a sphere with electrons scattered about in it, much as raisins are scattered about in plum pudding. Because of this, it became known as the plum pudding model of the atom (Figure 1.2). Since then, plum pudding has lost popularity. If Thomson's atom were named today, it might be called the blueberry muffin model with the blueberries representing the electrons.

Thomson's picture of the atom emerged from his work with cathode ray tubes. It was a milestone on the road to understanding atomic structure. But it was not the only major advance to come out of cathode ray experiments. Almost every television set in existence today is a cathode ray tube. The electrons stream from the cathode and are deflected by electromagnetic coils guided by signals from the television station. When an electron hits the television's screen, which is coated with a **phosphorescent** material, it produces a dot of color. The dots form the picture you see on the screen.

AN IMPROVED ATOMIC STRUCTURE

The plum pudding structure of the atom was short-lived. It was disproved by Ernest Rutherford, one of Thomson's best students. Rutherford was an unlikely scientist. He was born and raised in rural New Zealand, about as far as you can get from the world's scientific centers. He became interested in science while in elementary school. He did well at it immediately, winning scholarship after scholarship and degree after degree, all in physics or mathematics. At age 23, Rutherford got the job he wanted. He was awarded a fellowship to study at Cambridge. He elected to work with J.J. Thomson at the Cavendish Laboratory, the most advanced physics lab in the world.

Unlike his boss, Rutherford was a skilled experimentalist. His apparatuses were usually jury-rigged and crude, but they got the job done. His work with the particles and rays spontaneously emitted by **radioactive elements** led him to conclude that their emissions came in two forms. With admirable simplicity, Rutherford named them for the first two letters in the Greek alphabet, **alpha** and **beta**. After Cambridge, Rutherford accepted physics professorships at universities in Canada and Manchester, England, J.J. Thomson's hometown. He continued to work with radioactive materials. Rutherford was the first person to detect radon, a new element, and he made the startling announcement that radioactivity resulted from subatomic transformations that completely changed the nature of the atoms involved. When he won the 1908 Nobel Prize in Chemistry, Rutherford quipped that although he had witnessed many radioactive transformations, none occurred as quickly as his own—from physicist to chemist.

Rutherford accomplished all of this before he was 40 years old, but his best work was still to come. He was full of ideas. One of those ideas was to investigate further the atomic structure proposed by J.J. Thomson. Rutherford wanted to see what happened to alpha particles when they were fired at a thin sheet of gold foil. Rutherford knew that alphas were much bigger than electrons and that they carried a positive charge. The plum pudding atom, composed of a positively charged soup and tiny electrons, should not change the path of the more massive alpha particle. If the path of the alpha particles did not change after passing through the foil, it would add credence to the plum pudding model.

The apparatus was simple: a source of alpha particles, a sheet of gold foil, and a detection screen that glowed briefly whenever a particle struck it (Figure 1.3). The task was tedious: Count the number of glows (called **scintillations**) and note where on the detector they occurred. Rutherford assigned a student named Ernest Marsden to the boring chore. After observing thousands of scintillations, Marsden reported that some of the particles had been deflected by large amounts, and a few had bounced directly back toward the source of the radiation. It was, the surprised Rutherford said, like shooting cannon balls at a sheet of tissue paper and having some of them come back at you. Clearly, gold atoms contained something more massive than electrons, something that could make an alpha particle reverse direction upon impact.

This experiment eliminated the plum pudding model as a possible structure of the atom. But what did an atom look like? Rutherford figured that the only way to make alpha particles bounce backward

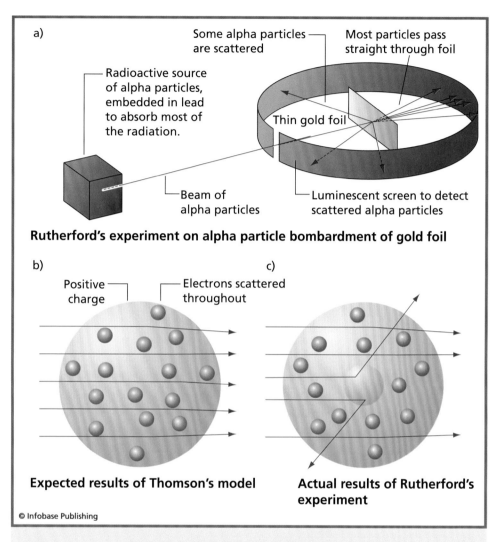

a)

Some alpha particles are scattered

Most particles pass straight through foil

Radioactive source of alpha particles, embedded in lead to absorb most of the radiation.

Thin gold foil

Beam of alpha particles

Luminescent screen to detect scattered alpha particles

Rutherford's experiment on alpha particle bombardment of gold foil

b)

Positive charge

Electrons scattered throughout

c)

Expected results of Thomson's model

Actual results of Rutherford's experiment

© Infobase Publishing

Figure 1.3   (a) Schematic of Rutherford's experiment to characterize the atom. (b) Expected results if J.J. Thomson's plum pudding model of the atom was correct. (c) Actual results. Some of the particles were deflected, indicating that the atoms contained something much more massive than electrons.

was for the gold atoms to have a dense positive charge. In a head-on collision, that charge would strongly repel the positively charged alpha particles. Also, because only a few of the bombarding particles were repelled, the atom's positive charge would have to be concentrated in a small space. Later—after more pondering, experimenting, and calculating—Rutherford announced his new structure of the atom. The atom was, he said, composed of a tiny positively charged nucleus with even tinier negatively charged electrons circling it. So small was the nucleus that if it were enlarged to the size of a marble and placed on the fifty-yard line of a football stadium, then the closest electron

PARTICLES, RAYS, AND WAVES

As scientists were probing the secrets of atoms, they were also cataloging the types of radiation some atoms emitted. But the names assigned to the different types of radiation were a bit confusing. The first emissions identified were called **X-rays** by Wilhelm Röntgen. He named them after the mathematical symbol for an unknown quantity. Cathode rays, which Rutherford called beta rays, turned out to not be rays at all but negatively charged particles that were later called electrons. Alpha radiation proved to be particles that are much more massive than electrons and carry a positive charge.

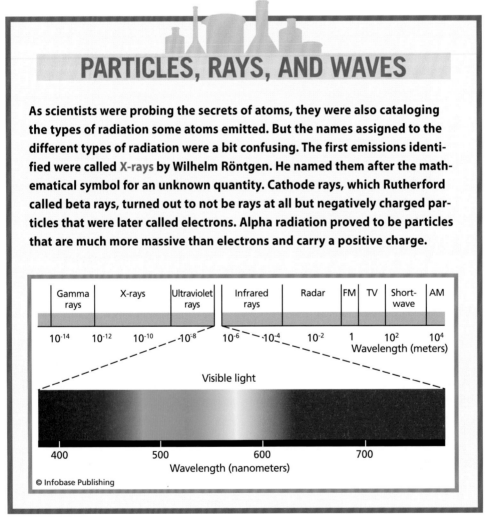

© Infobase Publishing

would be found in the upper decks. Atoms, it seemed, were mostly empty space.

The structure of the Rutherford atom was published in 1911. The new structure neatly fit the existing data, and it resembled a familiar arrangement: the solar system (Figure 1.4). Finally, two millennia after Democritus proposed the existence of atoms, scientists knew what Feynman's little particles looked like. Unfortunately, there was

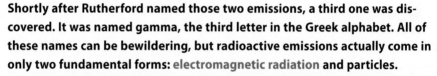

Shortly after Rutherford named those two emissions, a third one was discovered. It was named gamma, the third letter in the Greek alphabet. All of these names can be bewildering, but radioactive emissions actually come in only two fundamental forms: electromagnetic radiation and particles.

Electromagnetic radiation is pure energy, waves without any mass. Electromagnetic waves run from the highly energetic gamma and cosmic rays to low-energy radio waves. The rays in the visible part of the spectrum are called light waves.

Alpha and beta radiation, on the other hand, are particles that possess mass and charge. If we set the weight of a hydrogen atom as 1 and the charge on its ion as +1, then the table below gives the corresponding properties of the radioactive emissions known in the early twentieth century.

TABLE 1.1 TYPES OF RADIATION

RADIATION	WEIGHT	CHARGE
Alpha	4	+2
Beta	5.4×10^{-4}	-1
Gamma	weightless	electrically neutral
X-rays	weightless	electrically neutral

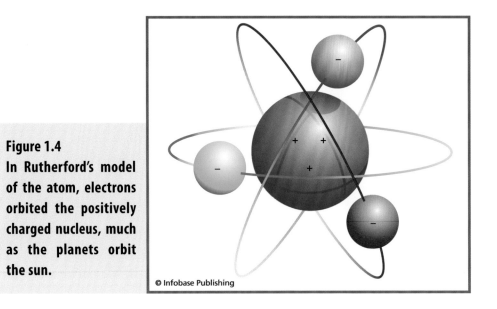

Figure 1.4
In Rutherford's model of the atom, electrons orbited the positively charged nucleus, much as the planets orbit the sun.

© Infobase Publishing

a problem. The laws of physics known at the time predicted that a negatively charged electron circling a positively charged nucleus would emit electromagnetic radiation, lose energy, and spiral down into the nucleus. According to the laws of physics, Rutherford's atom could not exist.

The Quantum Model

By the late nineteenth century, scientists had determined the fundamental laws of gravity, motion, electricity, magnetism, sound, optics, and heat. Physicists could predict the movements of the planets. They could calculate the speed of light. They understood the nature of heat. This knowledge allowed scientists and engineers to transform society. Trains replaced horses; steam engines did work once powered by human muscle. Many scientists believed in a clockwork universe. If one knew the position, speed, mass, and charge of every particle in the universe, one could predict the future. It would follow the present like, well, clockwork. By the beginning of the twentieth century, however, the fabric of the clockwork universe was fraying. The problem was three phenomena that were proving difficult to explain.

First was the blackbody problem. A **blackbody** is a theoretical object that emits and absorbs radiation. When heated, the intensity

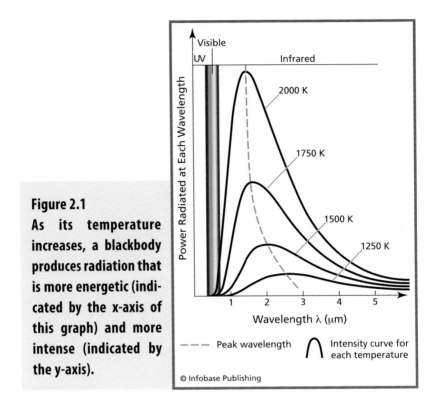

Figure 2.1
As its temperature increases, a blackbody produces radiation that is more energetic (indicated by the x-axis of this graph) and more intense (indicated by the y-axis).

and energy of its emitted radiation increases. Most solid objects—a fireplace poker, for example—closely mimic blackbodies. When a poker is heated in a fire, it first stays the same color, but heat is radiating from it in the form of infrared radiation. This radiation is invisible to our eyes but not to our hands. The usual response of anyone who touches a hot poker is a loud "ouch!" Heat the poker to a higher temperature, and it will turn red. The radiation is visible, because the poker is emitting higher energy waves, which our eyes can detect. This is true for any blackbody. Higher temperatures produce more energetic radiation of higher intensity, as shown in Figure 2.1.

This result was experimentally discovered in the nineteenth century, but it could not be explained by Maxwell's theory of electromagnetism. (James Clerk Maxwell was a Scottish physicist whose formulation of the laws of electricity and magnetism were published in 1871.) Try as they might, physicists could not come up with an equation that gave the results observed in blackbody radiation. One of the most prominent theories was based on the notion that a blackbody is composed of tiny oscillators. These oscillators produce a continuum of electromagnetic waves, analogous to the sound waves you get when you pluck the strings of a violin. But the spectrum predicted by this model and the experimental data did not fit well—and at the high energies of the ultraviolet range, the two did not fit at all. So serious was this breakdown of the laws of physics that scientists called it "the ultraviolet catastrophe."

An equally puzzling result was the **photoelectric effect**. When light of a single color (**monochromatic light**, or light of one wavelength) is shined on certain metals, electrons are knocked out of the metal. Maxwell's theory showed that light is an electromagnetic wave. However, the experimental results did not fit the theory. For example, when the light was moved closer to the metal, the intensity of the waves striking the metal increased. This meant that more energy was hitting the metal plate. More energy should produce more energetic electrons. In fact, although more electrons were knocked out of the metal, the energy of the electrons stayed the same no matter how bright the light was made. The physics of the day could not explain this and other aspects of the photoelectric effect.

Ernest Rutherford's proposed atomic structure added to the problems posed to nineteenth century physics by the ultraviolet catastrophe and the photoelectric effect. Rutherford's atom had a negatively charged electron circling a positively charged nucleus. The physics of the day predicted that the atom would emit radiation, causing the electron to lose energy and spiral down into the nucleus. Theory predicted that Rutherford's atom could not exist. Clearly, science needed new ideas to explain these three anomalies.

A QUANTUM LEAP

Max Planck, Albert Einstein, and Niels Bohr played the starring roles in solving the daunting problems that were facing physics at the beginning of the twentieth century. Each man won a Nobel Prize and all three are now deservedly installed in the pantheon of science. Of the three, the most unlikely one to revolutionize science was Max Planck, a physics professor at the University of Berlin. Planck was trying to come up with a mathematical expression that would account for the spectrum of blackbody radiation. He wanted desperately to resolve the ultraviolet catastrophe.

Although historians of science have studied the breakthrough that led to quantum mechanics, nobody can be exactly sure what was in Planck's orderly, disciplined mind when he devised the equation that revolutionized physics. He tackled the blackbody problem in several ways, but nothing worked. Finally, he tried an idea that was contradictory to all established concepts at the time: What if energy was not continuous? What if blackbodies absorbed and emitted it in little chunks? He wrote down his equation:

$$E = nhf$$

where E is the energy of the oscillators in the blackbody, n is the number of oscillators, f is the frequency of oscillation, and h is a very small number 6.6×10^{-34} **joule**-seconds, known today as Planck's constant. This is a very small number. In decimal form, it looks like this:

0.00000000000000000000000000000000066

Tiny, indeed, right?

When Planck used this relationship to calculate the spectrum of blackbody radiation, he came up with a result that agreed perfectly with experiment. More importantly, he had discovered quantum mechanics. Energy emitted by a blackbody is not continuous. Instead, it comes in tiny, irreducible packets or **quanta** (a word coined by Planck himself) that are proportional to the frequency of the oscillator that generated the radiation.

Planck presented his solution to the ultraviolet catastrophe at the December 1900 meeting of the Berlin Physical Society. No one grasped the implications of the breakthrough, probably not even Planck himself. His equation was considered to be a nice mathematical trick, but one with no particular physical significance.

One man who paid close attention to Planck's work was a young physicist working in a Swiss patent office. Albert Einstein was trying to explain the photoelectric effect. At the time, everyone knew that light was a wave, a continuous wave. But after reworking Planck's calculations, Einstein hypothesized that light might also be discontinuous. It might come in quanta, like the electromagnetic radiation emitted by blackbodies.

If light came in discrete packets, Einstein reasoned, then making the light brighter by moving the source closer to the metal would indeed knock more electrons out of the metal. But the energy of the packets (later named **photons**) from a monochromatic light source would stay the same. Thus, the energy of the ejected electrons would not change. This was exactly the result scientists had obtained experimentally. Einstein had explained the photoelectric effect. He had also demonstrated the quantum nature of light.

THE QUANTUM ATOM

The last big problem facing early twentieth century physics was Ernest Rutherford's atomic structure. Physicists knew that Rutherford's atom could not exist, but no one could come up with anything better. The man who would resolve this conundrum showed up at Manchester, England, in 1912 to work for Rutherford. Rutherford himself had worked for J.J. Thomson and had disproved Thomson's plum pudding structure of the atom. Now, the new man in Manchester, Niels Bohr, was about to do the same thing to Rutherford. By the end of his career, Bohr would have contributed as much as anyone to understanding Feynman's "little particles."

Science is a meritocracy. Poor kids can excel and get ahead in the world of science just as easily as the well-heeled. For example,

J.J. Thomson's father was a bookseller in the Manchester suburbs; Ernest Rutherford came from a rural, New Zealand family with no connections to the scientific world. Niels Bohr, on the other hand, was born with the equivalent of a scientific silver spoon in his mouth. He came from one of Denmark's prominent scientific families. His father was a respected professor of physiology. His mother was the center of a circle of intellectuals that met regularly at Bohr's home. Niels benefited early from his family's connections, receiving a gold medal for research he did in his father's lab while he was still a student. After getting his degree, he studied under J.J. Thomson in Cambridge. Then he went to work for Rutherford, one year after Rutherford had published the structure of his impossible atom. One problem above all interested Bohr: Why did an electron orbiting an atomic nucleus fail to obey the laws of physics? It was well known that opposite charges attract. So, what kept the negatively charged electron from spiraling down into the positively charged nucleus?

Bohr knew of the work of Planck and Einstein. What if the energies of electrons in an atom were not continuous? What if they could only take on certain values? What if atoms were quantized, just as blackbody oscillators and light that struck a metal plate were. The challenge was how to apply quantum ideas to the atom.

Bohr returned to Copenhagen when his fellowship at Manchester ran out. Nevertheless, he continued to think about atoms. The breakthrough came when he studied the spectrum of hydrogen. When hydrogen atoms are excited by an electrical discharge, they emit radiation. The emissions appear as sharp lines of radiation of specific wavelengths. Making use of a formula that described the spectrum of hydrogen developed by a Swiss schoolteacher named Johann Balmer, Bohr postulated a new structure for the hydrogen atom.

Like Rutherford, he pictured the atom as a tiny nucleus with an electron moving around it like a planet orbiting the sun. Bohr,

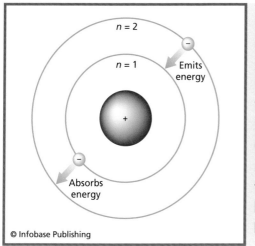

n = 2

n = 1

Emits
energy

+

Absorbs
energy

© Infobase Publishing

**Figure 2.2
By ejecting a photon (emitting energy), an electron can move from a higher to a lower energy level. Conversely, by absorbing energy, an electron can jump from a lower energy level to a higher one.**

however, postulated that each electron can only have certain energies. Consider a hydrogen atom with one electron and two energy levels. (Hydrogen actually has more than two energy levels, but we will consider only two in this example.) An electron can jump from a lower energy level to a higher one by absorbing energy from a photon or go from higher to lower by ejecting a photon (Figure 2.2). *But there are no intermediate energy levels. The atom is either in one state or the other and moves instantaneously between the two.*

Bohr's hypothesis solved the impossible atom problem. The energy of an electron in orbit was fixed. It could go from one energy level to another, but it could not emit a continuous stream of radiation and spiral into the nucleus. The quantum model forbids that.

Using Bohr's model, one could calculate the energy difference between orbits of an electron in a hydrogen atom with Planck's equation. In the example of a system with only two possible orbits, the equation of the emitted radiation as the electron went from a higher energy state E_2 to a lower one E_1 would be $E_2 - E_1 = hf$, where h is Planck's constant and f is the frequency of the emitted radiation.

Because hydrogen has more than two energy levels, it emits electromagnetic radiation at more than one frequency. Bohr's formulation accounted for all of hydrogen's emissions. Bohr pub-

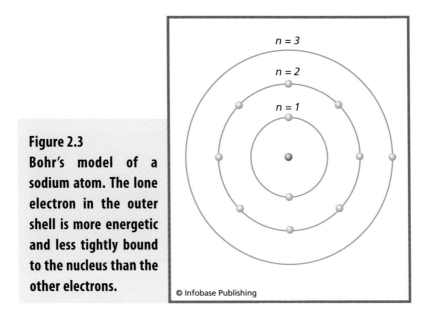

n = 3
n = 2
n = 1

Figure 2.3
Bohr's model of a sodium atom. The lone electron in the outer shell is more energetic and less tightly bound to the nucleus than the other electrons.

© Infobase Publishing

lished his quantized atomic structure in 1913. According to Albert Einstein, "it is one of the greatest discoveries."[2]

Hydrogen is the simplest atom: a positively charged nucleus with one negatively charged electron circling it. But what about helium? Or sodium? Or any of the heavier elements? Bohr knew his theory of the atom had to be extended to other elements. To account for the properties of other atoms, Bohr borrowed a concept originally introduced by J.J. Thomson. The idea was that electrons in atoms came in shells surrounding the nucleus. A shell can be thought of as an onion, with each layer of onion representing one shell.

Using this concept, Bohr could build imaginary atoms, electron by electron. He started with a nucleus. Then, one by one, he added electrons. After hydrogen came helium with a nuclear charge of +2. Helium is a very stable element, reluctant to lose or gain electrons. So, Bohr figured that two electrons would fill the first energy shell in an atom. Bohr then determined that it took eight electrons to fill the next energy shell. He continued until his atomic theory described all of the elements. Figure 2.3 shows Bohr's representation of a sodium atom.

The Bohr atom went a long way toward explaining the nature of atoms, but there were problems. Although scientists could calculate the emission spectrum of hydrogen using the Bohr model, the model could not account for the spectra of heavier atoms. The biggest problem with the Bohr atom, however, lay in its lack of a

INSTITUTE FOR THEORETICAL PHYSICS

Much of our understanding of quantum mechanics came out of a small building located near the soccer fields of Faelled Park in Copenhagen, Denmark. The building was constructed in 1921 to house Niels Bohr's new Institute for Theoretical Physics. The Institute became a magnet for aspiring physicists. One of the first to show up was Werner Heisenberg, who later won a Nobel Prize. Soon afterward came George Gamow, the fun-loving Russian physicist who sorted out the nuclear reactions that power the stars. Erwin Schrödinger, who also won a Nobel Prize in physics, stopped by to lecture on his new wave theory. Wolfgang Pauli, who would also win a Nobel Prize for his contributions to quantum mechanics, was there, too.

The atmosphere was informal. Ping-Pong and cowboy movies were favorite relaxations. But these were serious scientists working on the biggest shift in scientific thinking since Isaac Newton developed his laws of motion and gravity. The atmosphere was collegial but sometimes brusque. When Albert Einstein stopped by to argue with Bohr, he was treated like any other scientist. An example of this occurred one day after Einstein delivered a lecture on relativity. After he finished speaking, the teenager Wolfgang Pauli stood up. "You know," he said, "what Mr. Einstein said is not so stupid . . ."[3]

Great scientists came and went at the Institute. One thing remained constant, however: Bohr himself. He was kindly, brilliant, and well connected. Thus, it was only fitting that in 1965, on Bohr's birthday, the Institute for Theoretical Physics was renamed the Niels Bohr Institute.

solid theoretical foundation. The model explained nothing. What determines the energy levels of the electron orbits? Why are two electrons enough to fill the first energy shell in an atom, while eight electrons are required to fill the next one? While scientists struggled to understand the laws that governed Bohr's atom, other scientists were working on a different problem. That problem, when solved, would lead to a new structure that would replace Bohr's solar system model of the atom. The problem was light. Was it wave or particle?

BUILDING A NEW ATOM

More than 200 years ago, an Englishman named Thomas Young performed a set of experiments to establish the nature of light. The crucial one is known as the double-slit experiment. Figure 2.4 shows the setup. Light passes through a single slit or pinhole and continues on through a double slit. The result is a pattern of light and dark bands. When the peaks of two waves coincide, the result is a bright band of light; when the peak of one wave coincides with the trough of another, a dark band results because the two waves cancel one another out. Particles, however, do not have peaks and troughs, so this **interference pattern** would be impossible to produce if light were a particle. Later, Maxwell's theory reinforced Young's results. So, by the beginning of the twentieth century, scientists were certain that light was a wave.

One exception was Albert Einstein. His work in explaining the photoelectric effect indicated that light sometimes acted more like a particle. In fact, the key to understanding the photoelectric effect was that particles of energy called photons were kicking electrons out of a metal. This contradiction set Einstein to thinking deeply about light. Could light act as both particle and wave?

Einstein was cautious about this revolutionary idea. Furthermore, he was absorbed in sorting out another set of revolutionary ideas: the general theory of relativity. After clearing that up,

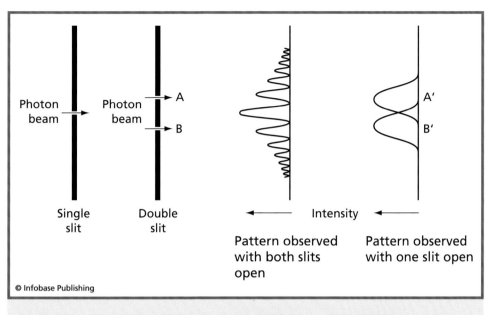

© Infobase Publishing

Figure 2.4   The double-slit experiment provided proof that light was a wave.

though, Einstein returned to the problems of quantum mechanics and finally accepted the hard-to-accept solution: Light had a dual nature—sometimes it acted like a particle, sometimes it acted like a wave.

As physicists wrestled with the concept of the dual nature of light, a young Frenchman named Louis de Broglie came up with an even bolder idea. If light could be both wave and particle, what about electrons? In fact, de Broglie hypothesized that all matter, from electrons to basketballs, has both wave and particle characteristics. But his equations showed that in larger bodies, bodies big enough to be seen by people, the wave character was negligible. This is why basketballs travel in a straight line toward the basket rather than in waves. Electrons, however, are small enough that wave characteristics play a large role in their behavior. De Broglie was unable to take his great insight further. That task would fall to a brilliant Austrian physicist named Erwin Schrödinger.

Just weeks after reading de Broglie's paper, Schrödinger produced his wave equation. The solutions to the wave equation gave the discrete energy levels used by Bohr and others to develop quantum mechanics. The discovery was a huge breakthrough because it provided a theoretical basis for the discontinuous energy levels of electrons in atoms. It gave quantum mechanics the sound foundation that had been missing. Another physicist, Werner Heisenberg (more about him later), produced a similar equation using an

EINSTEIN'S MIRACLE YEAR

Thousands of scientific papers are published each year. Most are quickly shoved into the dustbin of history to be retrieved, if at all, by highly specialized researchers working in the same area. A few will change the course of science. Only the best and most fortunate scientists will come up with one such paper in a lifetime. In a single year, 1905, Albert Einstein published three of them.

The papers concerned Brownian motion, the photoelectric effect, and the special theory of relativity. When very fine grains of pollen are mixed in water, the grains are not still in the water but move about in an erratic, trembling fashion. This unexplained effect is called Brownian motion. Einstein showed that Brownian motion was due to molecular collisions. After this paper, few could doubt the existence of molecules. Einstein's photoelectric hypothesis revealed the quantum characteristics of light and exposed its particle-like nature. Special relativity led to the insights that all motion was relative and that the speed of light was an absolute constant, no matter the speed of the light source relative to the point of measurement. A follow-up paper showed the relationship between mass and energy and led to the most famous equation of all:

$$E = mc^2$$

It was, indeed, a miracle year—not just for Einstein, but for science.

entirely different form of mathematics. Schrödinger's mathematics were easier to understand, so most physicists followed his lead. Using his equations, Schrödinger accurately predicted the spectrum of hydrogen.

Years later, physicists proved the wave character of electrons by producing the interference pattern predicted by de Broglie and first observed by Thomas Young in his experiments with light. Clinton Davisson and his junior partner Lester Germer in the United States and George Thomson in Great Britain made the discovery. For their work, Davisson and Thomson were awarded a Nobel Prize in 1937. Probably no other fact brings home the dual nature of matter better than this award. George Thomson was J.J.'s son. So J.J. won his Nobel for proving that electrons were particles. His son won for proving they were waves.

De Broglie's insight into the wave-particle nature of matter had a profound effect on scientists' picture of the atom. The solution to the wave equation led to an atom governed by probabilities. No longer could one say the electron is here or there. An electron in an atom could be anywhere, although some locations are more likely than others. This ambiguous character of electrons in an atom meshed well with the work of Werner Heisenberg. He showed that uncertainty was a fact of the atomic world. According to Heisenberg, one could not measure precisely both the position and the **momentum** of a particle. Although his famous **uncertainty principle** can be stated in many ways, the most common mathematical expression is

$$\Delta p \times \Delta q \geq h/4\pi$$

In this equation, the Greek letter delta, represents the uncertainties associated with the momentum p and the position q of a particle. The letter h is Planck's constant. The symbol $\geq$ means greater than or equal to. Thus, the product of the uncertainty associated with the momentum and position of any particle must be greater than or equal to Planck's constant divided by 4π. Fortunately, as noted earlier, Planck's constant is tiny, so the uncertainty principle plays no obvious role in our daily lives. But it is important for things the size of an atom.

This picture—the modern picture of the atom—is hard to accept. Electrons are both wave and particle; their position in an atom is governed by probabilities. If you ever do figure out exactly where one is, you cannot know its momentum. This is what the perceptive Professor Feynman said about the strangeness of reality at the atomic level in his book *Six Easy Pieces:*

> Things on a very small scale behave like nothing you have any direct experience about. They do not behave like waves, they do not behave like particles, they do not behave like clouds or billiard balls or weights on springs, or like anything that you have ever seen.

Of course, Feynman was right once again. To us oversized humans, the quantum mechanical world of the very small seems weird. However, quantum mechanics beautifully explains the behavior of atoms and predicts many oddities that have turned out to be true. Using quantum mechanics, many properties of atoms can be calculated. For example, chemists can now predict the shape of a **molecule** when atoms combine (molecules will be explored in more detail in Chapter 6). Another success was the prediction of the existence of a never-detected particle called the **positron**, a positively charged electron. Years after the prediction was made, experimental physicists discovered the particle.

The quantum world—however strange—is the atom's world. Quantum mechanics provides a powerful tool to probe the atom. Much of this book is devoted to using that tool to discover the properties of atoms, molecules, and compounds.

The Nucleus

A second sun, powerful and man-made, was born on July 16, 1945. A ball of fire thousands of times hotter than the surface of the real sun illuminated the New Mexico desert. Its birthplace was the Trinity site, and the explosion was the culmination of years of work by the world's brightest scientists. It was the planet's first atomic bomb, the tangible and frightening outcome of splitting the nucleus of an atom.

This spectacular result was the product of decades of research aimed at understanding the atomic nucleus. The quest began with Ernest Rutherford's early experiments, bombarding a sheet of gold foil with alpha particles. The atom, Rutherford concluded, was made up of two things: a tiny, heavy, positively charged nucleus surrounded by even tinier, and much lighter, negatively charged electrons. The nucleus of each element was unique. Iron had an iron nucleus; oxygen had an oxygen nucleus. Thus, the universe was composed of electrons and the 92 different nuclei of the elements. That picture would soon change dramatically.

DISCOVERY OF THE PROTON

Scientists were aware that particles other than electrons might exist. Cathode ray tube experiments had shown that something was moving in the opposite direction of the electrons. This new particle traveled from the positive anode to the negative cathode. This meant that it had a positive charge. Measurements showed that it was heavier than an electron but lighter than an alpha particle. Most scientists believed that the new particle was a hydrogen ion (a hydrogen atom minus its electron).

The first person to identify the hydrogen ion as a component of all atoms was Ernest Rutherford. Rutherford had his hand in virtually every aspect of atomic research. By 1919, he had discovered alpha and beta rays, found a new element (radon), won a Nobel Prize for his work with radioactive elements, and demonstrated that atoms had nuclei. For good measure, in 1914, he was knighted. However, still more discoveries and honors awaited him.

Rutherford began a series of experiments in 1917 that produced hydrogen ions when he shot alpha particles through air. One by one, he tested the components of air to find the source of the hydrogen ions. He finally shot the particles through an atmosphere of pure nitrogen. Surprisingly, he found that the number of hydrogen ions detected was greater in a nitrogen atmosphere than in ordinary air. The nitrogen was pure, with no hydrogen contaminants. Alpha particles have no hydrogen either. Rutherford had turned nitrogen into hydrogen, a process known as **transmutation**.

Over the next several years, Rutherford and other researchers bombarded assorted nuclei with alphas. Boron, sodium, and other elements all produced the same results: a hydrogen nucleus. This strongly suggested that the hydrogen nuclei were being knocked out of the nuclei of other elements. This meant that hydrogen ions were almost certainly present in all atoms. Rutherford named them **protons** from the Greek word meaning "first."

Rutherford continued to do research until his death, but the proton was his last big discovery. It was not, however, his last big honor. In 1931, the New Zealand country boy was raised to the peerage with the official name of Ernest, Lord Rutherford of Nelson. After his death six years later, he was awarded one last honor. He was buried in Westminster Abbey, where he keeps company with Isaac Newton and a handful of other great British scientists.

Rutherford's discovery of the proton did not radically change the picture of the atom, but it did present a problem. The atom was still thought to be made up of a heavy, positively charged nucleus surrounded by electrons. The difference was that scientists now knew that the nucleus was composed of protons. Measurements showed that the electrical charge of a proton was identical to, but opposite of, the charge on an electron. The proton's charge was positive, the electron's negative. Because atoms are electrically neutral, the number of protons in the nucleus had to equal the number of electrons. And that was the problem.

The atom closest in weight to hydrogen is helium. An atom of helium weighs four times as much as an atom of hydrogen. Rutherford's new model of the atom predicted that helium must have four protons, but helium was known to have only two electrons. Four positively charged protons plus two negatively charged electrons leave the helium atom with a charge of plus two. But helium, like all elements, carries no charge. Every element except hydrogen presented the same problem. One form of uranium, for instance, weighs 238 times as much as hydrogen but has only 92 electrons. Using Rutherford's model, uranium should carry a whopping net charge of +146 instead of the zero charge that it actually has. Much like Rutherford's first proposed atomic structure, his new atom, composed of protons and electrons only, could not exist.

Several theories were offered to make sense of Rutherford's new structure. Rutherford himself speculated that yet another particle, one that weighed the same as a proton but carried no charge, might lurk in the atomic nucleus. Over a decade would pass before the new particle was found.

DISCOVERY OF THE NEUTRON

James Chadwick was happy to return to England in 1917. He had been studying in Germany at the outbreak of World War I and had been imprisoned there for four years. He was broke but alive. Fortunately, his old mentor Ernest Rutherford took him in. His job was to search for the neutral particle that Rutherford believed must exist in the atomic nucleus, a particle he called a **neutron**.

Chadwick tried for years to produce a neutron. He blasted substances with alpha particles but always came up empty. His break came in 1932.

Irene Joliot-Curie (a daughter of Madame Curie, a pioneer in characterizing radioactive substances and the discoverer of radium) and her husband reported an unusual finding. Earlier experiments had shown that when beryllium was bombarded with highly energetic alpha particles, it emitted strong, electrically neutral radiation. The radiation was believed to be high-energy photons called gamma rays. The Joliot-Curies bombarded paraffin (a type of wax) with these mysterious beryllium rays and found that protons were ejected. As before, this result was interpreted to mean that the photons produced by the radiation were knocking protons out of the paraffin. This explanation made sense to the Joliot-Curies. Paraffin is rich in hydrogen, which they believed was the source of the emitted protons. This explanation is somewhat analogous to the photoelectric effect in which a photon of light ejects an electron from a metal. When

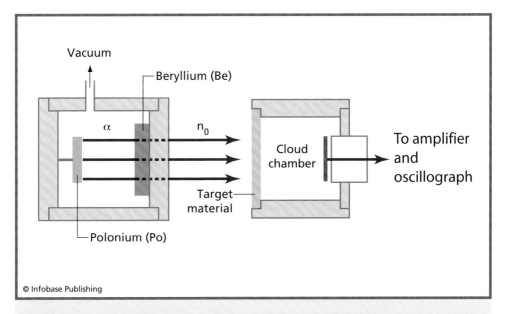

Figure 3.1   James Chadwick used the apparatus depicted above to discover the neutron. The polonium source emits alpha (α) particles. The particles strike a sample of beryllium, resulting in the emission of a neutron (n₀). The ejected neutrons hit the target material—paraffin, for instance—and eject a proton that is recorded by the detection device.

Chadwick reported this result, Rutherford shouted, "I do not believe it!"[4]

A proton weighs 1,835 times as much as an electron. Rutherford simply did not believe that a weightless photon would have enough energy to eject a particle as heavy as a proton. Yes, an energetic photon could kick out a much lighter electron, but not a proton. It would be like throwing a marble at a cannonball and expecting the cannonball to move. Chadwick immediately began to investigate the mysterious rays emitted by irradiated beryllium using the experimental set up shown in Figure 3.1.

Chadwick published his results in a short, classic paper in the British journal *Nature* under the title "Possible Existence of a Neutron." In the paper, he shows that high-energy photons (gamma rays) could not eject a proton from a nucleus. He wrote that the photon theory proposed by the Joliot-Curies could only be true "if the conservation of energy and momentum be relinquished at some point." Because these two conservation laws are bedrocks of physics, Chadwick had, ever so gently, dismissed the Joliot-Curies' explanation. He countered that the results of his experiments and those reported by the Joliot-Curies were what one would expect if the radiation emitted by the beryllium consisted of a particle with the mass of a proton but carrying no charge—in other words, a neutron.

ATOMIC NUMBERS

After Chadwick's discovery, scientists knew the three components of an atom: protons and neutrons in the nucleus with electrons hovering outside. The masses and charges of these constituents are shown in Table 3.1. Chemists have developed a system to describe the elements based on their atomic makeup. The atomic number of an atom is the number of protons in the nucleus. This number is usually represented by the letter Z. Thus, for hydrogen $Z = 1$, for helium $Z = 2$, and so on.

The weight of atoms and their constituents can be given in kilograms. A proton, for example, weighs 1.67×10^{-27} kilograms, but its weight or mass can be expressed more conveniently in a measure called the atomic mass unit (amu). One amu is defined as 1/12 the mass of a carbon atom that consists of six protons,

TABLE 3.1 **PROPERTIES OF THE COMPONENTS OF THE ATOM**			
PARTICLE	ELECTRIC CHARGE (E UNITS)	MASS (KILOGRAMS)	(ATOMIC MASS UNITS)
Electron	-1	9.109×10^{-31}	0.000549
Proton	+1	1.673×10^{-27}	1.00728
Neutron	0	1.675×10^{-27}	1.00867

six neutrons, and six electrons. A hydrogen atom would thus have an amu of about 1. The atomic number of an atom is given as a subscript and the mass as a superscript, both preceding the symbol for the atom. Thus, the form of carbon referred to earlier would be shown as $_{6}^{12}\text{C}$.

A glance at the **periodic table** (which will be covered in detail in Chapter 5) shows a list of elements with numbers that are not as neat as those for carbon. Iron, for instance, has an atomic mass of 55.845. Could an atom have a fractional proton or neutron? Of course not. An element must have a fixed number of protons. That is what defines it as an element. However, the number of neutrons in the nucleus of an element can vary. Carbon, for instance, has two prominent forms. Carbon 12 has 6 protons and 6 neutrons whereas carbon 14 has 6 protons and 8 neutrons.

Two forms of the same element are called **isotopes**. The isotopes of an element have the same atomic number but have different atomic masses. Iron has several isotopes that, when weighted by their naturally occurring abundance, gives an average mass of 55.845 amu. A simple example would be an element with only two isotopes, one with a mass of 10 amu, the other of 12 amu. If the isotopes were equally common, then the average atomic mass for that element would be 11. If 90% of the element occurred naturally as the isotope with a mass of 10 amu, then the average atomic mass would be 10.2, as calculated below:

$$(10 \times 0.9) + (12 \times 0.1) = 10.2$$

Using the new nomenclature, the nuclear reaction that led to Rutherford's discovery of the proton can be written as an equation:

$$_{7}^{14}\text{N} + _{2}^{4}\text{He} \rightarrow _{8}^{17}\text{O} + _{1}^{1}\text{H}$$

This equation says that a nitrogen nucleus is composed of seven protons and seven neutrons. An alpha particle, which is identical to a helium ion, has two protons and two neutrons. A highly energetic collision fuses the two nuclei. The result is a rare isotope of oxygen with eight protons and nine neutrons. The leftover proton is ejected. And that proton is what Rutherford detected.

RADIOACTIVITY

As early as 1902, Rutherford and his colleague, the chemist Frederick Soddy, realized that emissions of alpha and beta rays changed the nature of the emitting substance. One example of such a change is the spontaneous **radioactive decay** of the uranium-238 isotope, which emits an alpha particle and produces thorium:

$$^{238}_{92}U \rightarrow ^{234}_{90}Th + ^{4}_{2}He$$

Another example is when the lead-210 isotope decays to bismuth by emitting a beta particle:

$$^{210}_{82}Pb \rightarrow ^{210}_{83}Bi + e^-$$

In addition to these two common radioactive emissions, some isotopes emit neutrons when they decay. This usually happens with highly unstable isotopes. The degree of instability is measured by the isotope's **half-life**, which is the time it takes for

TABLE 3.2 A SAMPLING OF ISOTOPES

Element	Isotope	Half-life
Oxygen	^{16}O	∞
Uranium	^{238}U	4,460,000,000 years
Carbon	^{14}C	5,715 years
Silver	^{94}Ag	0.42 seconds

half of a sample of the isotope to decay. Start, for instance, with 1,000 atoms of isotope A that decays to isotope B. If the half-life of A is 1 day, then after 24 hours about 500 atoms of A and 500 atoms of B would be present. After another day, there would be about 250 atoms of A and 750 of B.

The half-lives of the elements vary widely, as shown in Table 3.2. Some isotopes, nitrogen-14 for example, are stable and experience no natural radioactive decay. However, bombarding even a stable element with energetic alpha rays can cause transmutation. Rutherford discovered the proton when he created hydrogen from a stable isotope of nitrogen.

Knowing the half-lives of the isotopes has helped scientists to better understand our world. The age of the Earth's earliest rocks has been estimated as 4.4 billion years based on the decay rate of uranium. Carbon dating, on the other hand, is of no value for dating ancient rocks, but its shorter half-life makes it useful for dating human artifacts, up to about 50,000 years old. Although scientists can measure the half-lives of hundreds of isotopes with great accuracy, mysteries remain. In a uranium sample, for instance, some atoms will decay today or tomorrow, but seemingly identical atoms will persist unchanged for billions of years. And no one knows why.

Mysteries such as this attract young people to science. Nuclear physics, however, tends to turn people off. Nuclear power plant malfunctions and atomic bombs are frightening. Nevertheless, humankind has greatly benefited from scientific investigations of the nucleus. Science's hard-won knowledge of the atomic nucleus is used extensively in medicine, from imaging procedures such as **positron emission tomography** (PET) to radiation therapy, which has saved the lives of many cancer patients.

HOLDING TOGETHER, BREAKING APART

By the 1930s, the structure of the atom worked out by Rutherford, Bohr, and others had answered the pressing questions fac-

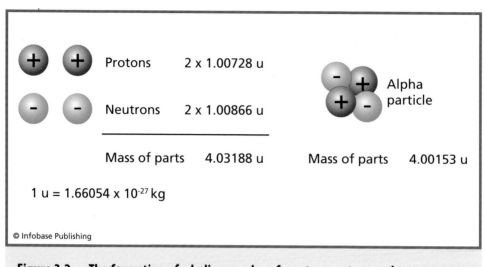

Protons	2 x 1.00728 u			Alpha particle	
Neutrons	2 x 1.00866 u				
Mass of parts	4.03188 u			Mass of parts	4.00153 u

1 u = 1.66054 x 10^{-27} kg

Figure 3.2   The formation of a helium nucleus from two protons and two neutrons results in a loss of 5 x 10^{-29} kilograms.

ing science at the beginning of the twentieth century. However, their picture of the atom had a flaw in it. Scientists knew that like charges repelled one another. The strength of that repulsion depends on the distance between the charged particles. The closer they are, the greater the repulsive force. How then could the two protons in a tiny helium nucleus stick together? Why don't they fly apart? What holds the 92 protons in uranium together?

The answer came in 1935 when the Japanese physicist Hideki Yukawa proposed that nuclei are held together by a new force, now called the **strong force**. The strong force operates only at very short distances. It has no effect until two particles are almost touching. Then they grab one another and hold tightly, a bit like a Velcro fastener. Because the strong force is, well, strong, it takes a lot of energy to break up a nucleus. That energy is called the **binding energy**. The more stable an element, the greater the binding energy between the atom's protons and neutrons (or **nucleons**).

The universal tendency of systems to seek their most stable state (the lowest energy state) drives an important nuclear event. When nuclei of light elements are fused, the new atomic nucleus weighs less than the sum of the weights of the particles that created the nucleus. Figure 3.2 shows how much mass is lost when two protons and two neutrons combine to form a helium nucleus. The lost mass comes from the system dropping to a more stable state and is manifested as energy. The amount of energy liberated is enormous. In fact, this fusion process is the reaction that powers the stars. Every photon of sunlight comes ultimately from the energy released when two protons and two neutrons fuse to form a helium nucleus. Fusion is perhaps the most important process in the universe. It is what makes life possible.

Understanding fusion invites another question: If fusing nuclei releases energy, how did the early atomic bombs work? In those bombs, nuclei were not fused, they were broken apart by nuclear fission. So, where does the energy of atomic bombs come from? An important piece of the answer came from a brilliant Jewish scientist who fled Nazi Germany shortly before World War II.

Lise Meitner was an Austrian-born physicist who worked in Germany. Because she was a woman, she was denied permission to work in the research lab and was relegated to the carpenter's workroom. Nevertheless, her hard work and diligent research earned the respect of her coworkers. When the Nazis took over, however, she was forced to flee to Sweden.

While trying to explain a puzzling result in some uranium experiments, a German colleague wrote Meitner and asked her to look at his data. Meitner, working with her cousin Otto Frisch, concluded that the strange results could only be explained by a splitting of the uranium nucleus to form two new elements. This process produces energy because the two atoms that are the products of the fission reaction are more stable than uranium, which means that they exist in a lower energy state. Thus, the reaction products weigh less than the uranium atom that spawned them. That weight loss is converted to energy.

The amount of energy created can be calculated with Einstein's equation, $E = mc^2$. In the equation, mass is multiplied by the speed of light in a vacuum squared. The speed of light is a huge number, and its square is even bigger. Consequently,

NUCLEAR MATH

Equations convey a lot of information concisely, but to get a deep sense for what an equation means, it is helpful to use it in a calculation. This is especially true with Einstein's relationship $E = mc^2$, where some numbers are huge and others are amazingly small.

Let's calculate the mass that was converted into energy in the first atomic bomb test. Measurements on the ground indicated that the explosive force of the bomb was equivalent to 37,200,000 pounds (16,874,000 kg) of TNT. That is so much TNT that scientists now measure atomic bomb explosions in kilotons (kt) of TNT. A kiloton is equal to 1,000 tons or 2,000,000 pounds (907,185 kg). Using the new units, the yield of the first bomb would be:

$$\frac{37,200,000 \text{ lb}}{2,000,000 \text{ lb/kt}} = 18.6 \text{ kt}$$

Let's use the international metric system units for this calculation. In this system, the energy (E) is given in joules (J). A joule is the amount of work done that will produce the power of one watt continuously for one second. It is roughly the amount of energy required to lift one kilogram 10 centimeters. Mass (m) in the equation is in kilograms, and the speed of light (c) is in meters per second.

To find the mass converted in the explosion, we rearrange the equation to:

$$m = E/c^2$$

the energy produced by converting even a small mass of a substance is huge. If one gram of matter were converted to energy, it would provide enough power to lift a million tons of water from sea level to the top of Pikes Peak—twice. The calculation in the sidebar on pages 40-41 shows how much mass is required for an atomic bomb like the one that produced a second sun in New Mexico.

$$c = 3.0 \times 10^8 \text{ meters/second}$$
$$c^2 = 9.0 \times 10^{16} \text{ meters}^2/\text{sec}^2$$

Now convert the energy of the explosion from kilotons to joules and calculate the mass:

$$1 \text{ kt} = 4.18 \times 10^{12} \text{ J}$$
$$18.6 \text{ kt} = 7.8 \times 10^{13} \text{ J}$$

However, 1 joule is defined as 1 kg*m^2*s^{-2}, so

$$m = E/c^2 = 7.8 \times 10^{13} \text{ kg*m}^2\text{*s}^{-2}/9.0 \times 10^{16} \text{ m}^2\text{*s}^{-2}$$
$$m = 8.6 \times 10^{-2} \text{ kg}$$

or

$$m = 0.86 \text{ g}$$

One can think of mass as "frozen energy." As this calculation shows, a tiny bit of mass can liberate an enormous amount of energy. Less than a teaspoon of it can—and did—level a sizable city, as was demonstrated dramatically by the atomic bomb dropped on Hiroshima in 1945.

The Electrons

When the energy in the nucleus of an atom is released, the results are spectacular. Atomic bombs and reactors that power entire cities grab everyone's attention. But most of the everyday world is governed by an atom's electrons, the swirling cloud of negatively charged matter that can act as particles or waves.

The properties of most substances—from steel to stones, from light bulbs to tulip bulbs—are largely determined by the number and energy of the electrons in the atoms making up the object. This chapter will explore how electrons are arranged in an atom and how scientists discovered those arrangements.

ENERGY SHELLS

Niels Bohr proposed that electrons were particles that circled a nucleus in shells that determined their energies. Helium, he knew, has two electrons. It is a very stable atom, one that refuses to gain or lose electrons under most conditions. Bohr concluded that two electrons filled the lowest energy shell.

Electrons in atoms heavier than helium, Bohr hypothesized, must go into higher energy shells. Thus, lithium, with an atomic number of 3, has two electrons in the $n = 1$ energy shell, and the third electron must go into a new energy shell with $n = 2$.

The number of electrons required to fill an atom's energy shells was first worked out by extending Bohr's ideas about helium to the other noble (or inert) gases. All of these gases are very stable. They do not react with other substances easily. This means that they do not gain or lose electrons readily. As early as 1916, Bohr and others suggested that these gases must have energy levels that are filled and can take no more electrons. Table 4.1 shows the electron configurations of the noble gases. Scientists now know that Bohr and his colleagues were right. All of the lowest energy shells of every noble gas are filled.

Bohr's electron configurations were a logical outgrowth of his quantum atomic structure. In many ways, the Bohr atom was a remarkable success. Over time, however, problems arose. Higher-resolution spectroscopes revealed new lines in the hydrogen spectrum. Bohr's atom could not explain this so-called "fine structure." Nor could it explain the spectra of atoms larger than hydrogen. The biggest problem with the Bohr atom, though, lay in its empirical

TABLE 4.1 ELECTRONIC CONFIGURATIONS OF NOBLE GAS ATOMS							
ELEMENT	ATOMIC NUMBER *(Z)*	NUMBER OF ELECTRONS IN ENERGY SHELL *(n)*					
		1	2	3	4	5	6
Helium	2	2					
Neon	10	2	8				
Argon	18	2	8	8			
Krypton	36	2	8	18	8		
Xenon	54	2	8	18	18	8	
Radon	86	2	8	18	32	18	8

nature. What was magic about the number of electrons required to fill the energy shells of the noble gases? Why did two electrons satisfy $n = 1$ shells? Why did it take eight to fill $n = 2$ shells? These questions were not answered until Heisenberg and Schrödinger developed wave mechanics.

QUANTUM NUMBERS

Today, scientists know that the energy and behavior of electrons in an atom are determined by a set of four quantum numbers. The wave function of Schrödinger's equation reduces to three equations. The solution to these equations yields the first three **quantum numbers** and the limits on the values they can have. The first of these is the **principal quantum number** *(n)*. Following the convention that began with Bohr's atom, the principal quantum number for the lowest energy shell is $n = 1$, the next is $n = 2$, and so on where n is any positive whole number or **integer**. The higher the principal quantum number, the greater the energy of the electrons in that shell.

Quantum numbers can be considered to be approximately equivalent to physical features in the atom proposed by Bohr. The principal quantum number corresponds to one of Bohr's circular energy shells. It is related to the average distance of the electrons from the nucleus. Electrons with larger n values are more energetic and farther from the nucleus.

The second quantum number is called the **angular momentum quantum number**. It is designated by the letter ℓ and can be thought of as representing a subshell within a principal energy

TABLE 4.2 LETTER DESIGNATION OF THE SUBSHELLS	
VALUE OF ℓ (SUBSHELL)	**LETTER**
0	*s*
1	*p*
2	*d*
3	*f*
4	*g*

TABLE 4.3 ALLOWABLE ORBITALS IN THE PRINCIPAL ENERGY SHELLS *(n)* OF AN ATOM			
n	ORBITAL INTEGER *(ℓ)*	ORBITAL LETTER	ORBITAL NAME
1	0	*s*	1*s*
2	0	*s*	2*s*
	1	*p*	2*p*
3	0	*s*	3*s*
	1	*p*	3*p*
	2	*d*	3*d*
4	0	*s*	4*s*
	1	*p*	4*p*
	2	*d*	4*d*
	3	*f*	4*f*

shell. This quantum number governs the angular momentum of the electrons and determines the shape of an **orbital**, which indicates where an electron is likely to be in the atom. The angular momentum quantum number can be any positive integer between 0 and n–1. For example, up to three orbitals could be present in an energy shell with a principal quantum number of 3 ($n = 3$). They would have angular momentum quantum numbers of $\ell = 0$, $\ell = 1$, and $\ell = 2$.

Angular momentum quantum numbers are usually designated by the letters given in Table 4.2. The convention for identifying orbitals includes the number of the principal energy shell. A hydrogen electron in its **ground state** (or lowest energy level) would occupy a 1*s* orbital, where the 1 specifies the principal quantum number and the *s* denotes the angular momentum quantum number. If the electron jumped to the next higher energy level, its orbital would be called 2*s*. Similarly, the lowest energy *p* orbital would be 2*p*. Table 4.3 shows which orbitals are allowed in the first four principal energy shells of an atom.

The third solution to Schrödinger's equation produces the **magnetic quantum number**, usually designated as m_ℓ. Allowable values of this quantum number range from $-\ell$ to $+\ell$. A summary of

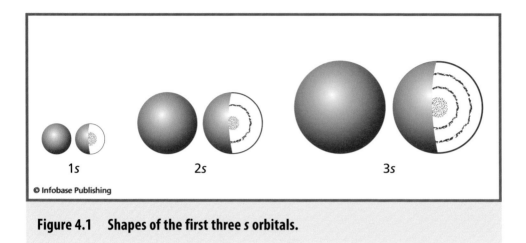

Figure 4.1   Shapes of the first three *s* orbitals.

the possible values allowed by the wave equation for the first four quantum numbers is shown in Table 4.4. The magnetic quantum number specifies how the *s*, *p*, *d*, and *f* orbitals are oriented in space.

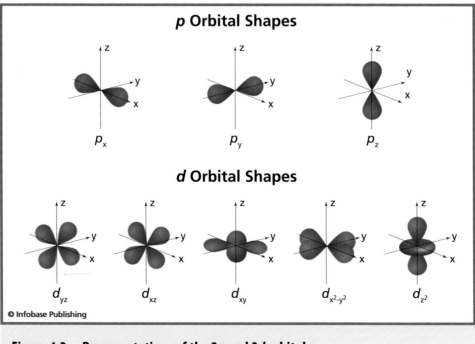

Figure 4.2   Representations of the 2*p* and 3*d* orbitals.

The shapes of the first three s orbitals are shown in Figure 4.1. The orbitals are spherical, with the lower-energy orbitals nested inside the higher-energy orbitals.

Figure 4.2 shows the p and d orbitals. The p orbitals are dumbbell shaped, and all but one d orbital have four lobes. The orbital shapes represent electron probabilities. The chance of finding an electron within the boundary of an orbital is approximately 90%.

The last quantum number was proposed to solve a mystery. Some spectral lines split into two lines when theory predicted that only one should exist. Several physicists had a hand in trying to solve this problem. By 1924, a consensus was reached. A new quantum property and number were needed to explain spectral splitting. At the time, the electron was considered to be a particle, and scientists called this new property "spin," usually designated as m_S. The spin quantum number has only two possible values $+1/2$ or $-1/2$. It is usually depicted as an arrow pointing up or down.

TABLE 4.4 ALLOWABLE QUANTUM NUMBERS FOR THE FIRST FOUR ENERGY SHELLS

PRINCIPAL QUANTUM NUMBER (n)	ANGULAR MOMENTUM QUANTUM NUMBER (ℓ)	ORBITAL SHAPE DESIGNATION	MAGNETIC QUANTUM NUMBER (m_ℓ)	NUMBER OF ORBITALS
1	0	1s	0	1
2	0	2s	0	1
	1	2p	-1, 0, +1	3
3	0	3s	0	1
	1	3p	-1, 0, +1	3
	2	3d	-2, -1, 0, +1, +2	5
4	0	4s	0	1
	1	4p	-1, 0, +1	3
	2	4d	-2, -1, 0, +1, +2	5
	3	4f	-3, -2, -1, 0, +1, +2, +3	7
LIMITS OF QUANTUM NUMBERS				
$n = 1, 2, 3 \ldots$	$\ell = 0, 1, \ldots (n-1)$		$m_\ell = -\ell \ldots, 0, \ldots +\ell$	

The spin quantum number brings up a question: What physical features of the atom do the quantum numbers represent? The answer is ambiguous because of the way quantum numbers were derived.

Quantum numbers were first developed for the Bohr atom when electrons were thought to be charged particles orbiting a nucleus. As mentioned earlier, the principal energy quantum number corresponds to the average energy of the electrons in a shell of the Bohr atom. The angular momentum quantum number is associated, not too surprisingly, with the angular momentum of an electron in an elliptical orbit. The magnetic quantum number is related to the behavior of electrons in a magnetic field. Spin can be visualized as an electron spinning on its own axis.

After the wave theory supplanted the Bohr atom as a more accurate description of the subatomic world, the meaning of quantum numbers became less certain. Can a wave really spin on its own axis? The answer is no. It is sometimes useful to think of quantum numbers as conferring concrete, physical characteristics to an electron. But quantum properties are only fuzzily related to things in the normal, human-sized world. Thus, electron spin has no ordinary physical meaning. Electrons do not spin like tops—or anything else. Feynman hit the nail on the head when he wrote in *Six Easy Pieces*: "Things on a very small scale behave like nothing you have any direct experience about." Everything scientists have learned about electrons bears Feynman out.

BUILDING ATOMS

The principal quantum number establishes the average energy of the electrons in an energy shell. Electrons in the orbitals (or sub-shells) of a principal energy shell have different energies. For the $n = 3$ energy shell, the energy of every electron in the 3s, 3p, and 3d orbitals is slightly different. To build atoms, it is necessary to know why.

A helium atom has two protons and two electrons, twice as many of each as hydrogen. Since positive charges attract negative charges, the nucleus of helium should exert twice as much force on its electrons as hydrogen does. This means it should be twice as hard to remove an electron from a helium atom than it is to remove one from hydrogen. But it is not. Instead of twice as much energy, it takes only about 1.9 times as much.

Extracting an electron from helium takes less energy than expected because of electron-electron repulsion. The helium nucleus actually does pull twice as a hard as a hydrogen nucleus does, but the two electrons in helium are also repelling one another. The net effect is to make an electron in a multielectron atom easier to remove than one would expect if the other electrons were not present.

A diagram showing the energy levels of the atomic orbitals is shown in Figure 4.3. In some cases, the energy of an outer orbital in a lower principal energy level is greater than that of an inner orbital in a higher principal energy level. A 4*d* orbital, for instance, has higher energy than a 5*s* orbital. This is unexpected. It happens because electrons in the 4*d* orbital are repelled by the electrons in the inner *s* orbitals. Consequently, it takes less energy to remove an electron from a 4*d* orbital than it would take to remove one from the 5*s* orbital.

Knowing the energy levels of the orbitals enables us to begin building the periodic table—atom by atom. The lightest atom is hydrogen, which has one proton and one electron. So, into which orbital should that electron go? The answer, as we have seen, is in a 1*s* orbital. But why? Why not a 2*p* or 5*d*? The answer comes from a rule postulated by Niels Bohr back in the 1920s when he was building the atoms of the periodic table using his new, quantized atomic structure. It is called the **Aufbau principle**. This principle is the first of three rules needed to build atoms. It states simply that lower-energy orbitals fill first. Looking at Figure 4.3,

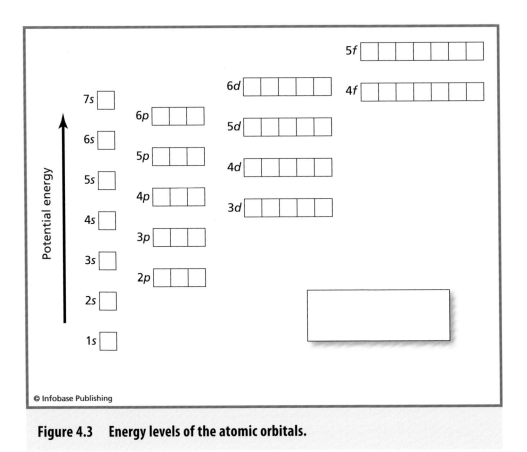

Figure 4.3   Energy levels of the atomic orbitals.

it is clear that the $1s$ orbital has the lowest energy. Therefore, the electron must go there. Helium, the next lightest element, has two electrons. According to the Aufbau principle, they, too, would go in the $1s$ orbital.

The next element is lithium, with three electrons. But the third electron does not go in the $1s$ orbit. The reason it does not arises from one the most important rules in quantum mechanics. It was devised by Wolfgang Pauli (and would result in a Nobel Prize for the Austrian physicist). The rule Pauli came up with is called the **Pauli exclusion principle**; it is what makes quantum numbers so crucial to our understanding of atoms.

The exclusion principle states that no two electrons in an atom can have the same set of quantum numbers. The 1s orbital has the following set of allowable numbers: $n = 1$, $\ell = 0$, $m_\ell = 0$, $m_S = +1/2$ or $-1/2$. All of these numbers can have only one value except for spin, which has two possible states. Thus, the exclusion principle restricts the 1s orbital to two electrons with opposite spins. A third electron in the 1s orbital would have to have a set of quantum numbers identical to those of one of the electrons already there. Thus, the third electron needed for lithium must go into the next higher energy shell, which is a 2s orbital.

The final complication in building atoms comes when we reach carbon. Carbon's most common form has six electrons. To build this atom, the first two electrons go in the 1s orbital, the second pair in the 2s orbital. The fifth electron must go the 2p orbital. But in which of the three p orbitals should the sixth electron go? In the orbital already occupied by the fifth electron or in one of the unoccupied orbitals.

The last rule needed to generate electron configurations for all the atoms in the periodic table came from a German scientist named Friedrich Hund. **Hund's rule** can be expressed in several ways. The most precise definition is that atoms in a higher total spin state are more stable than those in a lower spin state. Thus, the sixth electron in carbon-12 must have the same spin as the fifth one. The Pauli exclusion principle then requires that it fill an empty p orbital.

Knowing these three rules—the Aufbau principle, the Pauli exclusion principle, and Hund's rule—and the energy levels of the orbitals shown in Figure 4.3, one can build the correct electron configurations of most atoms. Chemists specify electron configurations by first identifying the principal quantum number, then the orbital, and finally the number of electrons in that orbital. The electron in a hydrogen atom would be 1s^1, carbon-12 would be 1s^2 2s^2 2p^2. Table 4.5 shows how orbitals are progressively filled from hydrogen to neon.

Electron configurations get more complicated with higher atomic numbers. One example is the **transition elements**, which have atomic numbers 21 to 30. Electron repulsion causes the $4s$ orbital to be slightly less energetic than the $3d$ orbitals, making the $4s$ orbital fill first. So, the electron configuration for vanadium, atomic number 23, is $1s^2\, 2s^2\, 2p^6\, 3s^2\, 3p^6\, 3d^3\, 4s^2$. But when an electron is added to vanadium to get chromium, it does not go into the unfilled $3d$ orbital to produce an atom with two outer orbits of $3d^4$ and $4s^2$. Instead, the new electron and an old one from the $4s$ orbital shift to the $3d$ orbital. This means that the two outermost orbitals of chromium are $3d^5$ and $4s^1$. This is chromium's most stable state. The five unpaired electrons in the d orbitals and one unpaired electron in the s orbital are a lower energy configuration

TABLE 4.5 ORBITAL NOTATIONS

CHEMICAL SYMBOL	ATOMIC NUMBER	ORBITAL NOTATION			ELECTRON CONFIGURATION NOTATION
		$1s$	$2s$	$2p$	
H	1	1			$1s^1$
He	2	1⌊			$1s^2$
Li	3	1⌊	1		$1s^2\, 2s^1$
Be	4	1⌊	1⌊		$1s^2\, 2s^2$
B	5	1⌊	1⌊	1	$1s^2\, 2s^2\, 2p^1$
C	6	1⌊	1⌊	1 1	$1s^2\, 2s^2\, 2p^2$
N	7	1⌊	1⌊	1 1 1	$1s^2\, 2s^2\, 2p^3$
O	8	1⌊	1⌊	1⌊ 1	$1s^2\, 2s^2\, 2p^4$
F	9	1⌊	1⌊	1⌊ 1⌊1	$1s^2\, 2s^2\, 2p^5$
Ne	10	1⌊	1⌊	1⌊ 1⌊ 1⌊	$1s^2\, 2s^2\, 2p^6$

MAXIMUM ELECTRONS IN ORBITALS AT A PARTICULAR SUBLEVEL

$s = 2$ (one orbital)

$p = 6$ (three orbitals)

$d = 10$ (five orbitals)

$f = 14$ (seven orbitals)

than the $3d^4$ and $4s^2$ that one would expect. This is Hund's rule at work. The six unpaired electrons in chromium give a lower-energy atom than the expected configuration.

Fortunately, most electron configurations follow the normal filling sequence. Much of the data that enabled scientists to understand electron configurations came from a branch of science barely touched upon so far. That science is **spectroscopy**, and it has played a key role in understanding how electrons behave in atoms.

SPECTROSCOPY

Electron configurations are crucially important in chemistry. They determine how atoms combine to form the everyday materials around us, such as water, wood, and plastics. However, most of the electron configurations examined so far are a special case. They are the arrangements found in atoms in the ground state, their most stable, lowest-energy state.

When atoms absorb a photon, an electron leaves the ground state for a more energetic orbital. When the electron drops to a lower-energy orbital, it gives out energy, often in the form of a photon. Spectroscopy is the branch of science that investigates that quantum of emitted or absorbed radiation.

The science of spectroscopy is rooted in the work of Joseph von Fraunhofer, a German physicist. He separated sunlight into its component colors using high quality **diffraction gratings** and prisms. In 1814, he discovered hundreds of dark lines in the sun's spectrum, now called Fraunhofer lines. He could not, however, explain their source. Scientists know now that the lines are caused by elements near the sun's surface absorbing radiation produced in the sun's interior.

Analysis of spectra such as Fraunhofer lines is called absorption spectroscopy because it deals with atoms capturing a photon that bumps an electron into a higher energy state. Emission spectroscopy uses an external source of energy—heat, radiation, or an electrical current, for instance—to excite the electrons in an atom. When the electrons fall from an excited, higher-energy state to a lower energy level, they emit a photon. Spectroscopists measure the wavelength of the emitted photons. Using Planck's equation, they can calculate the energy released in the transition.

By the early twentieth century, scientists had analyzed the spectra of most elements. They knew that each element produced a characteristic emission spectrum. Because hydrogen is the simplest atom, much of the research to understand the nature of atomic spectra centered on it.

Send an electric current through a glass tube containing hydrogen at low pressure and a blue light will appear. When this light passes through a prism, four colored lines show up—red, blue-green, blue, and violet. Because this series of lines is in the visible range, it was discovered in the early days of spectroscopy. A Swiss physicist named Johann Balmer developed an equation in 1885 that enabled him to calculate the wavelengths of the lines. This is the same equation that Bohr used to postulate the quantum nature of the hydrogen atom. Balmer's equation also predicted the existence of other spectral lines for hydrogen, including one near the edge of the visible spectrum, which was detected soon afterward. To honor his contributions to spectroscopy, this series of spectral lines is called the Balmer series.

The discovery of two other series of emission lines of hydrogen came later. They are named for their discoverers: the Lyman series in the ultraviolet range and Paschen series in the infrared region. Although formulas were devised to calculate the spectral lines, the physics behind the math was not understood until Niels Bohr proposed his quantized atom. Suddenly, the emission spectrum of hydrogen made sense. Each line represented the energy released when an excited electron went from a higher quantum state to a lower one.

Over time, scientists sorted out the electron transitions that produce every line in the spectrum of hydrogen (Figure 4.4). The high-energy Lyman series comes from transitions to the ground state of hydrogen, $n = 1$. The less energetic Balmer series in the visible region involves electrons dropping to the $n = 2$ energy level. The low-energy Paschen series in the infrared region comes from electrons going into the $n = 3$ energy level. The reason more energy is emitted when electrons transition to the $n = 1$ level is that the

JULY 4TH SPECTROSCOPY

The simplest form of emission spectroscopy is called flame spectroscopy. Flame spectroscopy can be used to identify some common elements. No fancy equipment is needed. The best way to do flame spectroscopy is to use a platinum loop. This piece of standard laboratory gear consists of a fine, 2-inch (5.1-cm) platinum wire twisted into a loop and embedded in a 4-inch (10.2-cm) glass rod. The only other lab equipment needed is a Bunsen burner or its equivalent.

Dissolve a pinch of table salt (sodium chloride) in water. Dip the platinum loop in the solution and stick it in the flame. The result is a bright yellow glow. The color comes from two yellow emission lines that dominate the spectrum of sodium. The emission lines result from electrons dropping from the 3p to the 3s orbital. The two lines are very close to one another. The difference in energy is due to the slightly different energies of the electrons in the 3p orbital because of their spin.

Solutions of the chlorides of copper, lithium, barium, and many other metals also give off bright colors in a hot flame. Copper is a distinctive blue, lithium a glowing red, and barium a nice shade of green. These metals do their thing on the 4th of July when the fireworks begin. The spectacular clouds of color come from electrons in metal atoms dropping into lower energy orbitals. It is a grand display of flame spectroscopy.

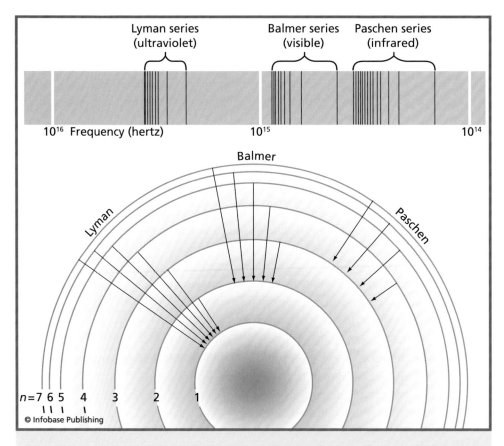

Lyman series
(ultraviolet)

Balmer series
(visible)

Paschen series
(infrared)

10^{16} Frequency (hertz) 10^{15} 10^{14}

Balmer

Lyman

Paschen

$n=7\ 6\ 5\quad 4\quad 3\quad 2\quad 1$

© Infobase Publishing

Figure 4.4   The lines in the hydrogen spectrum correspond to the emission of energy when an electron drops to a lower energy level.

difference in energy levels increases as n gets smaller. Thus, a large dollop of energy is emitted when electrons transition to the $n = 1$ level, but less energy is emitted in transitions into higher energy levels, such as $n = 2$ or $n = 3$.

Spectroscopy continues to play important roles in chemistry, physics, and astronomy. Easy-to-use spectrometers enable chemists to rapidly identify the elements. Common **organic molecules** also have characteristic emission and absorption lines, making spectroscopy an invaluable tool for analyzing complex chemicals.

Spectroscopy has also been a key to understanding the universe. Astronomers attach spectrometers to their telescopes to study the makeup of the sun and the stars and to measure their speeds relative to Earth and one another. In fact, spectroscopy is one of science's most valuable tools. It owes a huge debt to the many experimenters who recorded the spectral lines of hundreds of elements and compounds. But their work is the superstructure that rests on the solid foundations laid by Bohr, Schrödinger, and their colleagues.

The Elements

The periodic table orders the elements in a way that helps chemists understand why atoms behave as they do. What makes fluorine react violently with cesium while its nearest neighbor neon is reluctant to react with anything? In other words, what gives the elements their properties and what order lies below the surface of their seemingly random nature? Scientists know now that the periodicity of the elements is due largely to recurring patterns in their electron configurations.

The periodic table orders the elements in columns, rows, and blocks. The elements in a column are called a group. Group 1 elements are in the column on the far left of the periodic table. Group 2 elements are in the next column. The progression continues to Group 18 on the far right. The elements in a column have very similar properties. The elements in blocks or rows have a few similar characteristics, but they are not as closely related as the elements in a column.

Periodic tables can be constructed that contain many different kinds of data. The table on page 110 includes the symbol, atomic number, and atomic mass of each element. The table on page 112 includes the electron configurations. Let's begin with the electron configurations.

The system of notation used in this periodic table to spell out electron configurations is based on the noble gases—unreactive elements with filled electron shells. The first noble gas is helium. Thus, the electron configuration of lithium, the next heaviest element, is shown as [He]$2s^1$. This means that lithium has the electron configuration of helium plus one additional electron in the $2s$ orbital. Molybdenum ($Z = 42$) has an electron configuration [Kr]$5s^14d^3$. Thus, molybdenum has the electron configuration of krypton plus one electron in the $5s$ orbital and three in $4d$ orbitals. The electron configurations of all the elements are depicted this way. Looking closely, some interesting similarities between the elements become apparent.

The electron shells of all the elements in Group 1, for instance, are filled, except for a single electron in an outermost s orbital. In fact, most of the elements in any column of the periodic table have the same number of electrons in their outermost orbitals, the orbitals involved in chemical reactions. Those orbitals are usually the same type orbital—s, p, d, or f, though there are a few exceptions. As mentioned in Chapter 4, vanadium ($Z = 23$) has an unexpected quirk in the arrangement of the electrons in its outer orbitals. Platinum ($Z = 78$) exhibits a similar anomaly, as do a few other elements. Most elements, however, play by the rules. This is why the elements in a group behave similarly.

One of the key concepts clarified by the discovery of electron configurations was an idea that had been around chemistry for a long time—the idea of **valence**. Historically, valency was associated with the eagerness of elements to combine with one another. After electron configurations became known, valence came to mean the number of electrons an atom must lose or gain to complete the its outermost orbital. This led to a related term—valence electrons. Valence electrons are the electrons in an atom's outermost orbital. Valence electrons govern how atoms combine with one another to form compounds. Atoms gain or lose electrons in their outer orbitals because it

NAMING ELEMENTS

The names of all the elements and their symbols are shown in the tables in the back of this book. Most of the symbols match up with the names: H for hydrogen, O for oxygen, C for carbon, He for helium, Li for lithium. Symbols for the newer elements are easy to interpret, too. Element 101, for instance, has the symbol Md and the well-deserved name of Mendelevium. But a few of the symbols in the periodic table do not match the names of their elements. Sodium, for instance, does not have the symbol So. Instead, it is Na. Potassium isn't Po, but rather K.

The reason for this dysfunctional arrangement lies in the history of the elements. Some elements acquired names that are no longer used, but the symbols live on in the periodic table and in chemical formulas. The name for element number 19 is potassium, which came from the English word for potash. Potash is potassium carbonate, K_2CO_3, which is a source of potassium. The name potash comes from the old practice of preparing the chemical by leaching wood ashes in pots. It is not clear who pinned the name kalium on potassium, but it may have been the Germans. Potassium is called kalium in German, a word derived from the Arabic word for ash. The word kalium is long gone from the English language, but its first letter is still around as the symbol for potassium.

The following ten elements, whose original names were Latin words, also have mismatched names and symbols:

Sodium, Na (natrium)   Antimony, Sb (stibium)
Iron, Fe (ferrum)   Tungsten, W (wolfram)
Copper, Cu (cuprum)   Gold, Au (aurum)
Silver, Ag (argentum)   Mercury, Hg (hydragyrum)
Tin, Sn (stannum)   Lead, Pb (plumbum)

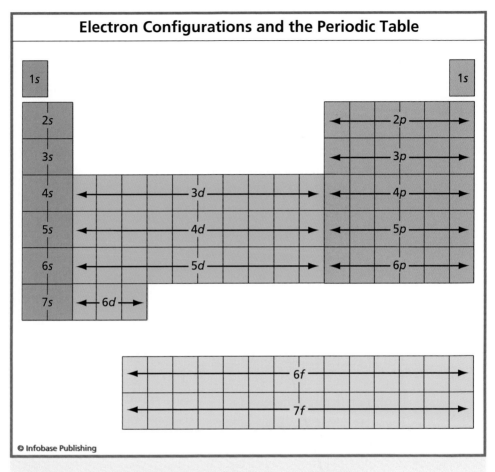

Figure 5.1   **Blocks of elements with the same outer orbitals.**

moves them toward a stable, lower-energy state like those of the noble gases. This topic will be investigated further in the next chapter.

In addition to columns, rows and blocks of elements in the periodic table also have features of their electron configurations in common. Figure 5.1 highlights blocks of elements with the same outer orbitals. As you move from left to right in a row within a block, it shows which orbital is being filled. However, the elements in a row have a different number of electrons in their outer orbital. Consequently, adjacent elements in a row might have something in common with one another, but their chemical behavior is not as uniform as that found in the elements of a group.

In addition to having similar electron configurations, some blocks have common chemical characteristics, too. The block of elements on the far left of the illustration, for example, are all metals. The two groups in the block are called the **alkali metals** (first column) and **alkaline earth metals** (second column). The alkali metals are remarkably similar: soft, silvery, highly reactive metals. The alkaline earth metals form another distinctive group that are much harder that the alkaline metals and have higher melting points.

Classifying the elements by physical and chemical characteristics enabled scientists to assemble periodic tables long before their electron configurations were known. In fact, the first periodic table came before J.J. Thomson discovered the electron and long before Bohr developed electron configurations.

THE FIRST PERIODIC TABLE

The science of chemistry languished until Robert Boyle—a brilliant, fanatically religious man—wrote *The Sceptical Chymist* in 1661. He gave scientists a new way of seeing the world by defining an element as any substance that could not be broken down into a simpler substance, an idea that closely coincides with today's notion of an element. Boyle's insight led chemists into their labs, where they heated solids and evaporated liquids and analyzed the gases that boiled off and the residues that remained behind. They isolated a flood of new elements.

Two centuries later, chemists had identified 63 of the 92 naturally occurring elements. But they had no useful way of organizing them, no system that would allow them to understand the elements' relationship to one other. Did the elements have any order? The question stumped the world's best chemists until the Russian scientist Dmitri Mendeleyev solved the problem in 1869. His eureka moment did not come in his lab but in his bed. "I saw in a dream," he wrote, "a table where all the elements fell into place as required."[5] He called this arrangement the periodic table, a copy of which adorns virtually every chemistry classroom and textbook on the planet.

By explicitly showing the relationship between the elements, Mendeleyev was able to predict the existence and properties of elements that had not yet been discovered. He theorized, for example, that an undiscovered element should fall between silicon and tin on the periodic table. In 1880, German chemist Clemens Winkler isolated a new element, which he named germanium, that had exactly the properties that Mendeleyev predicted.

The best-known photograph of Mendeleyev shows him in his later years. He looks like a brooding madman, with a long white beard and a shock of wiry hair that a local shepherd trimmed once a year with sheep shears. But Mendeleyev was not a madman; he was a brilliant chemist who contributed valuable insights in many areas of science until his death in 1907.

Despite his numerous achievements, Mendeleyev is remembered mainly for the periodic table. Central to his concept was the conviction that the properties of the elements are a periodic function of their atomic masses. Today, chemists believe that the periodicity of the elements is more apparent when the elements are ordered by atomic number, not atomic mass. However, this change affected Mendeleyev's periodic table only slightly because atomic mass and atomic number are closely correlated. The periodic table does not produce a rigid rule like Pauli's exclusion principle. The information one can extract from a periodic table is less precise. This is because its groupings contain elements with similar, but not identical, physical and chemical properties.

PERIODIC FEATURES OF THE ELEMENTS

One seemingly obvious relationship in the periodic table is the one between atomic number and atomic size. Clearly, as the number of protons and electrons in an atom increases so should the atomic radii. Unfortunately, it's not that simple. A glance at Figure 5.2

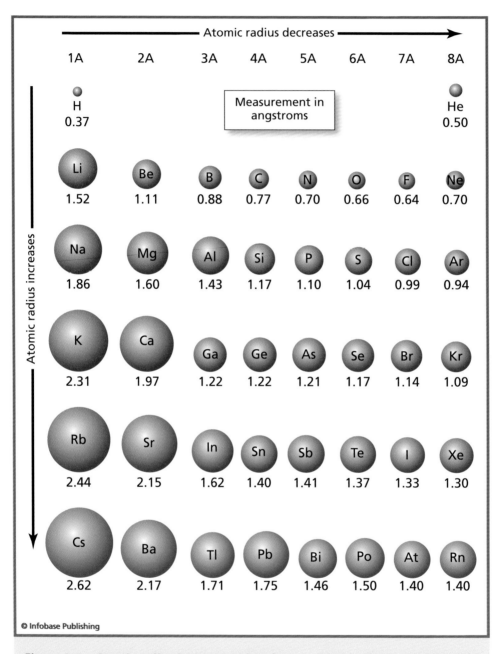

Figure 5.2 **Atomic radius increases going down a column of the periodic table and generally decreases going across a row.**

confirms the problem. Atomic radii do increase as expected in the vertical groups. In Group 1, for example, lithium ($Z = 3$), sodium ($Z = 11$), potassium ($Z = 19$), and on down all have increasing atomic sizes. This is expected because as one goes down the group, the elements are adding principal energy shells ($n = 1, 2, 3 \ldots$). The average distance of the electrons from the nucleus increases with increasing values of n.

The horizontal rows confound that simplicity. Instead of size increasing with atomic number, it usually *decreases*. The reason is that as one goes from left to right along a row, the number of positively charged protons in the nucleus increases. For most elements in most rows, though, the principal energy level stays the same. The result is a nucleus with a higher positive charge that pulls the electrons in more tightly. Electron repulsion tends to offset the increased attraction by the nucleus, but in most cases, it is not enough to balance the increased force exerted by the nucleus on the electrons.

Ionization Energy

The **ionization energy** of the elements is another important property with periodic characteristics. Remove one or more electrons from an atom and you get an ion. The energy required to remove electrons from an atom in the gaseous state is called the ionization energy. First ionization energy is the energy required to remove one electron from an atom, specifically the highest energy electron, the one bound least tightly to the nucleus. Second ionization energy is the energy needed to remove the most energetic electron remaining in the atom after the first one is gone—and so on.

First ionization energies generally increase as one moves from left to right along a row in the periodic table. They tend to decrease from the top to the bottom of a group. This is the same pattern exhibited by atomic radii. It gets harder to remove an electron as you move from left to right because the increasing nuclear charge tends to hold them more tightly. Within vertical groups, though, the increased nuclear charge is offset by electron repulsion and higher principal energy levels; it gets easier to remove an electron as one goes down the group. These trends are summarized in Figure 5.3.

Ionization energies are important indicators of how atoms behave in chemical reactions. Atoms with low first ionization energies, such as sodium, give up an electron easily. This means they form ions readily. Carbon, on the other hand, has a first ionization energy that is twice as large as that of sodium; it does not give up electrons as willingly. This difference in first ionization energies has a dramatic impact on the chemical properties of the two elements. Sodium reacts with chlorine to form sodium chloride, table salt, a white crystalline material that dissolves in water. Carbon

MEASURING ATOMS

Measuring the radii of atoms is not a walk in the park. Electrons in atoms are neither here nor there. They are merely more likely to be here than there. Measuring the size of an atom is a bit like measuring the size of a cotton ball. The answer depends on how much you decide to compress it. Similarly, the size of an atom depends on how one chooses to measure it.

To accommodate this problem, scientists have come up with several approaches to measuring atomic sizes. A common one is called the covalent radius, which is half the distance between the nuclei of two identical atoms. This technique works well for atoms such as hydrogen or oxygen, both of which readily pair up to form H_2 and O_2. But how would one determine the covalent radius of a noble gas, which exists only as single atoms?

One solution, the one adopted in this book, is to ignore the measurement difficulties and use radii calculated by standard quantum mechanical methods. This approach yields consistent values for the atomic radii of all the elements.

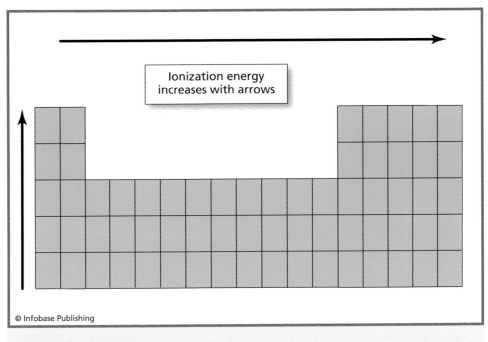

Ionization energy
increases with arrows

© Infobase Publishing

Figure 5.3   First ionization energies generally increase across a row and tend to decrease going down a column.

combines with chlorine to form carbon tetrachloride, a colorless liquid once used in fire extinguishers. It does not dissolve in water, and it is toxic—do not sprinkle this chloride on your food. In other words, carbon tetrachloride is about as different from table salt as day is from night. One reason is the big difference in the ionization energies of sodium and carbon. This difference determines the type of the bond between the two elements, which strongly affects the properties of the resulting compound.

The group whose elements have the lowest ionization energies is the alkali metals, which easily lose an electron. The group with the highest ionization energies is the noble gases, which have filled energy shells and strongly resist losing or gaining electrons. After the noble gases, the elements that cling most tightly to their electrons are their next-door neighbors in Group 17 of the periodic table. The elements in this group are called the **halogens**. The two elements most eager to react and exchange an electron are francium at the bottom left of the periodic table and fluorine at the top of the halogen group. Francium is highly radioactive and quite rare. Less than a kilogram of francium exists at any given instant in all of the Earth's crust. The element with the next lowest first ionization energy is cesium. Cesium wants to give up an electron and fluorine wants one badly. Consequently, when cesium and fluorine are brought together, the result is what chemists like to call a "vigorous reaction." Others might call it an explosion.

Electronegativity

The last periodic characteristic of the elements considered here is **electronegativity**. Electronegativity is almost the exact reverse of ionization energy. Ionization energy is a measure of how hard it is to remove an electron from an atom. Electronegativity measures the tendency of an atom to attract electrons. The two numbers are arrived at differently, however. Ionization energy is a property of an atom in the gaseous state. Electronegativity is a property of an atom when it is joined to another atom in a chemical bond.

The periodic nature of the electronegativity of the elements is shown in Figure 5.4. Electronegativity generally decreases going down a group and generally increases going from left to right in a row. Francium is the least electronegative element; fluorine is the most.

Like valency, the concept of electronegativity has been around a long time. However, it was not an especially useful idea until 1932 when the two-time Nobel Prize–winning chemist Linus Pauling developed a method to quantify the electronegativity of the elements. Pauling's approach was to assign a value of 3.98 to fluorine, the most electronegative element. Most tables of electronegativity round this number off to 4.0. Pauling then calculated the electronegativity of the other elements based on this value for fluorine. The electronegativity scale ranges from a low of 0.7 to a high of 4.0.

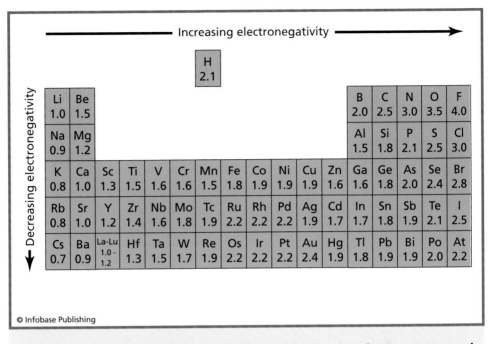

Figure 5.4 **Electronegativity generally decreases going down a group and generally increases going from left to right in a row.**

The difference in the electronegativity of two elements chemically joined in a compound determines the nature of the bond between them. When two elements with similar electronegativity combine, they tend to share an electron. In a carbon-carbon bond, for example, the two atoms would share valence electrons equally. Bonds of this sort are called **covalent** bonds. Two elements with similar electronegativities, such as carbon and chlorine, would form covalent-like bonds. But elements with greatly different electronegativities would tend to have an electron closer to one atom than the other. In the cesium fluoride example, fluorine wants to grab an electron to fill its outermost orbital, and cesium is barely holding on to one in its outermost orbital. When the two combine, the electron migrates from cesium to fluorine. The resulting bond is called an **ionic bond**. As was the case in comparing table salt with carbon tetrachloride, the nature of the bond between two atoms—ionic or covalent—plays a big role in determining the properties of the resulting compound. Both ionic and covalent bonding will be covered in the next chapter.

Chemical Reactions: Making Molecules

The previous chapter explored the elements—their electron configurations, their periodicity, and their properties. This chapter will investigate how chemists create more complex substances—the bits of matter called molecules.

Molecules are combinations of atoms. A substance composed of one proton and one electron is a hydrogen atom. When two hydrogen atoms bond together they form a hydrogen molecule, H_2, the normal form of hydrogen in the atmosphere. Hydrogen is the simplest molecule, with an amu of about 2. Some molecules, especially those assembled in living organisms, can be huge. Hemoglobin, for instance, the oxygen-transport molecule that keeps all humans and other mammals alive, has over 4,600 hydrogen atoms in it. It also has 2,953 carbon atoms, not to mention a smattering of nitrogen, oxygen, sulfur, and iron atoms. Add them together and the result is a huge molecule of about 65,000 amu.

The processes that create molecules, from tiny to huge, are called **chemical reactions**. A reaction occurs when two or more atoms or molecules form new molecules. Saying it in a different way, a chemical reaction occurs when a chemical transformation or change takes place. When two hydrogen atoms unite to form H_2, a chemical reaction has occurred. When cesium and fluorine "react vigorously," a chemical reaction has taken place. Many different chemical reactions have to happen for your body to manufacture a complex molecule like hemoglobin.

Some of the changes that occur around us are not chemical changes, but changes in the state of the same molecules. Water, ice, and steam are quite different in appearance and behavior, but they are all made up of H_2O molecules. Table salt is a white crystalline substance until you add water to it and the solid disappears, but no chemical reaction has taken place. What's dissolved in the water is still a form of sodium chloride. Evaporate the water and what's left is what you started with—table salt.

Chemical reactions can be divided into two types. **Exothermic reactions** are those that give off heat when they react. These are reactions where the heat content of the reactants is greater than the heat content of the reaction products. Cesium reacting with fluorine is a highly exothermic reaction. The other type of chemical reaction is called an **endothermic reaction**. These reactions soak up heat as they proceed, cooling the local environment. The most famous—and the most important—endothermic reaction on Earth is photosynthesis, which converts water and carbon dioxide into glucose and oxygen. This reaction is not a **spontaneous reaction**, which is one that proceeds naturally without requiring added energy after the reaction is initiated. Photosynthesis would not occur without the addition of energy. The energy that drives it is electromagnetic radiation from the sun.

Many chemical changes are **reversible reactions**. Burning carbon in the form of coal, for instance, is highly exothermic. Oxygen atoms combine with carbon to produce carbon dioxide and heat. But passing carbon dioxide over a bed of hot carbon causes an endothermic reaction that partially reverses the process, removing an oxygen atom from carbon to make carbon monoxide. Water exhibits the same reversibility. Burning hydrogen in air produces water and heat. Applying energy to water in the form of an electric current dissociates the H_2O, producing hydrogen and oxygen. This process is known as **electrolysis**.

Many exothermic reactions are spontaneous. A critical question facing chemists in the late eighteenth century was how to tell spontaneous reactions from nonspontaneous ones without performing an experiment. What characteristics must the reactants have to proceed without the prod of added energy? In other words, what drives chemical reactions?

The answer came from an American, a man who entered Yale College at age 15 and was awarded the first Ph.D. in engineering ever given in the United States. Although Josiah Willard Gibbs is not well known outside of scientific circles, he was one of America's most accomplished theoretical physicists. His career would be considered unusual in today's highly mobile world. Gibbs was born in New Haven, Connecticut, in 1839; he died there in 1903. All of his degrees came from Yale, his hometown college, and he spent most of his life as a professor at the school. Perhaps never straying far from home allowed Gibbs the time to think through the knotty problem of what makes chemicals react spontaneously. In any case, he came up with the answer: a quantity known today as **Gibbs free energy**.

PREDICTING REACTIONS

Gibbs free energy is the energy available to do work. The Gibbs free energy of a closed system, a system where neither matter nor energy can be added or escape, can be represented in the equation

$$G = H - TS$$

where G is the Gibbs free energy of the system, H is the system's **enthalpy** or heat content, S is the **entropy** (a measure of randomness or disorder), and T is the **absolute temperature**. With this equation, one can calculate the Gibbs free energy of any system. But that knowledge is not very valuable without the key insight that goes with it:

Every system seeks to achieve a minimum
of free energy.

In chemical reactions, one or more substances are transformed into something new. If the "something new" has a lower Gibbs free energy than the reactants, the reaction will proceed spontaneously—as with cesium and fluorine. If not, then energy must be added for the reaction to take place as in photosynthesis. An easy way to understand this is to consider a system with two possible states, x_1 and x_2. The states have an associated Gibbs free energy of G_1 and G_2. State x_1 is the initial unreacted state; x_2 is the state following a chemical reaction. If G_1 is greater than G_2, then the reaction will proceed from state 1 to state 2 in order to reach the state with the lower Gibbs free energy. If G_1 is less than G_2, then no reaction will occur unless energy is added to the system. This can be stated more concisely in mathematical form as:

$$G_2 - G_1 < 0 \text{ Favors reaction}$$
$$G_2 - G_1 > 0 \text{ Does not favor reaction}$$

where < is the mathematical symbol for "less than" and > means "greater than." If $G_2 - G_1 = 0$, the two states are in **chemical equilibrium** with one another.

Calculations of Gibbs free energy usually assume that the reaction takes place at constant temperature. Thus, it can be written as

$$G_2 - G_1 = H_2 - H_1 - T(S_2 - S_1)$$
or
$$\Delta G = \Delta H - T\Delta S$$

The units normally used in calculating the change in Gibbs free energy are the usual SI (Système International d'unités) units. The Gibbs free energy is given in kilojoules per mole; the enthalpy in joules per mole per kelvin (the kelvin is the unit of temperature used in the absolute temperature scale; 1 kelvin is equal to 1 degree Celsius), and the temperature in kelvin. To make the numbers easier to use, a new unit of measurement is introduced here. It is called the **mole**, also known as the gram molecular mass of a substance.

CHILLING OUT

Chemical reactions are not the only processes governed by the Gibbs equation. Solids will dissolve spontaneously in liquids only if the Gibbs free energy change is negative. As in chemical reactions, the process can be either exothermic or endothermic. Adding sodium hydroxide to a beaker of water will produce a strongly exothermic reaction. As the white powder dissolves, it liberates enough heat to burn the hand holding the beaker. Endothermic processes are usually less vigorous but equally interesting.

When ammonium nitrate, NH_4NO_3, dissolves in water, it absorbs heat. Consequently, its standard enthalpy of solution must be positive. This means that the entropy change caused by ammonium nitrate going from solid to solution must increase for the process to proceed spontaneously. This is exactly what one would expect based on the concept of entropy as a measure of randomness or disorder.

Solid ammonium nitrate is an orderly, crystalline substance, a state considerably less random than a solution of ions in water. In this case, the positive entropy change outweighs the enthalpy change. That is $T\Delta S > \Delta H$. The Gibbs free energy change is negative, so the process will proceed spontaneously.

Many of the cold packs sold in stores use this endothermic process. A cold pack usually contains a flimsy plastic bag of solid ammonium nitrate inside a larger package filled with water. When punched, the inner bag ruptures. This releases the ammonium nitrate, which dissolves and produces a chilled pack to relieve pain and swelling in aching joints.

The idea of a mole started in 1811 with a remarkable insight by the Italian physicist Amadeo Avogadro. Avogadro correctly assumed that molecules were tiny distinct entities. This led him to hypothesize that equal volumes of gases at the same temperature and pressure contained the same number of molecules, no matter what the molecule was. One could fill two beakers of equal size with two different gases—one with hydrogen, for example, and the other with carbon dioxide. Then, if the gases in both beakers were at the same temperature and pressure, the number of hydrogen molecules in the first beaker would equal the number of carbon dioxide molecules in the second beaker. Furthermore, if the beaker were the right size to hold 2 grams of hydrogen, which is the gram molecular equivalent of a hydrogen molecule's mass in amu, that beaker would contain 1 mole of hydrogen. If the same beaker had 1 mole of carbon dioxide (CO_2) in it, the weight of the gas would be

$$1 \text{ carbon (amu = 12)} + 2 \text{ oxygen (amu = } 2 \times 16)$$
$$= 44 \text{ grams}$$

A mole of a substance is independent of volume. A mole of hydrogen in a beaker could be compressed to half its size and it still would be a mole of hydrogen. A mole is not a measure of volume or weight. A mole of hydrogen weighs much less than a mole of carbon dioxide. A mole is exactly what Avogadro said it was two centuries ago: a measure of the number of bits of matter, usually molecules, in a gram molecular mass of that substance. In the late nineteenth century, scientists devised techniques for determining that number. Today's best estimate is that there are 6.02×10^{23} atoms or molecules in a mole.

Now, let's return to the Gibbs free energy equation to determine if hydrogen will react spontaneously with oxygen to form water. The equation for the reaction may be written as

$$H_2 + \tfrac{1}{2}O_2 \rightarrow H_2O$$

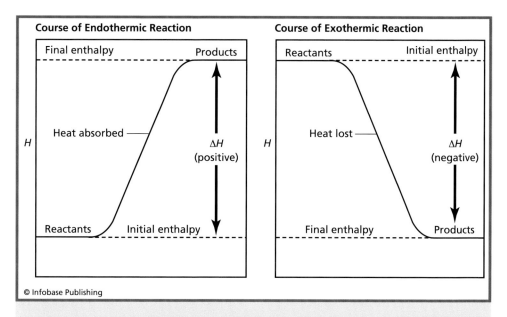

Figure 6.1   In an endothermic reaction, the heat content of the products is greater than the heat content of the reactants. In an exothermic reaction, the heat content of the reactants is greater than the heat content of the products.

First, one must determine if this is an exothermic reaction. Gibbs equation states that an exothermic reaction must have a negative value of ΔH. This means that the heat content of the reactants is greater than the heat content of the products. The difference in heat content between the two states is released during the reaction as the system goes to a lower energy state. The opposite is true of an endothermic reaction, as is shown in Figure 6.1.

The standard **heat of formation** of a substance is the enthalpy change involved in forming 1 mole of it from its elements. The standard heat of formation is measured at 25°C (or 298 K) and one atmosphere of pressure for gases or 1 **molar solutions** for liquids. Tables of the heat of formation are usually given in units of kilojoules per mole. For water, the standard heat of formation is -286 kJmol^{-1}. The minus sign means that the reaction is exothermic and heat is given off.

Enthalpy change is only half of the Gibbs equation. The other half accounts for any entropy change caused by the reaction. The entropy change, ΔS, can be calculated from tables that give the entropy of many simple substances. These are usually not tables of the entropy of formation but of total entropy. And, unlike the enthalpy tables, the units are in joules per mole per kelvin, not kilojoules. One can calculate ΔS by subtracting the total entropy of the products of the reaction from the entropy of the reactants. This gives an entropy change for the hydrogen-oxygen reaction of -164 Jmol^{-1}K^{-1}. So, the Gibbs equation now looks like

$$\Delta G = \text{-286 kJmol}^{-1} - [(T)(\text{-164 Jmol}^{-1}\text{K}^{-1})]$$

Because all of the data in this equation were determined at the standard temperature of 25°C or 298 K, the result is

$$\Delta G = \text{-286 kJmol}^{-1} - [(298)(\text{-164 Jmol}^{-1}\text{K}^{-1})]$$
$$\text{or } \Delta G = \text{-286 kJmol}^{-1} + 49 \text{ kJmol}^{-1}$$
$$\Delta G = \text{-237 kJmol}^{-1}$$

Solving the Gibbs equation reveals a great deal about the reaction of hydrogen and water. First, because ΔG is negative, one knows that the reaction will proceed spontaneously. Because the enthalpy is negative, the reaction must be exothermic. The entropy change, however, is negative. This means that the entropy of the reactants is greater than that of water. This is not surprising. Entropy is a measure of randomness. Gases tend to be more random than liquids, which are more random than solids. At 25°C, hydrogen and oxygen are gases, while the product of the reaction, water, is liquid. Thus, entropy should, and does, decrease.

Expanding on this example, some general criteria for predicting chemical reactions are possible. From the example, one can see that the enthalpy component in the calculation is much larger than the entropy component. This is usually (but not always) true. With this conclusion and the information from the Gibbs equation, we can formulate four qualitative rules for predicting the likelihood that a chemical reaction will take place, even if we do not know the change in Gibbs free energy. These are shown in Table 6.1.

Now, let's return again to the reaction between hydrogen and oxygen. The reaction is exothermic, and the change in heat content overwhelms the smaller entropy decrease, making it a spontaneous reaction. Anyone who has seen the heart-stopping photographs of the burning of the hydrogen-filled zeppelin *Hindenburg* knows just how vigorously hydrogen reacts with oxygen. Yet, if one mixes hydrogen and oxygen together in the lab, the two elements will intermingle and not react at all. What's going on?

Many reactions proceed like hydrogen and oxygen. The reactants coexist peacefully until a bit of energy is added to the system. Coal, for instance, will not heat a house until someone lights the kindling. The *Hindenburg*, the world's largest airship, was brought down by a chemical reaction between hydrogen and oxygen, ignited most likely by a single spark. The added energy needed to initiate some chemical reactions is called the **activation energy**.

Why do hydrogen and oxygen require a spark before they will react? To react with one another, the oxygen molecule O_2 and

TABLE 6.1 HOW CHANGES IN ENTHALPY AND ENTROPY AFFECT REACTION SPONTANEITY

ENTHALPY CHANGE	ENTROPY	SPONTANEOUS REACTION?
Decreases (exothermic)	Increases	Yes
Increases (endothermic)	Increases	Only if unfavorable enthalpy change is offset by favorable entropy change
Decreases	Decreases	Only if unfavorable entropy change is offset by favorable enthalpy change
Increases	Decreases	No

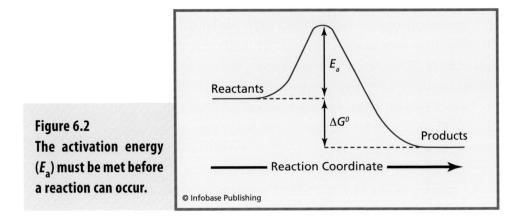

Figure 6.2
The activation energy
(E_a) must be met before
a reaction can occur.

the hydrogen molecule H_2 must be broken down into the atomic forms, O and H. In a mixture of the two gases at room temperature, the **kinetic energy** of the molecules is not sufficient to break the oxygen-oxygen and hydrogen-hydrogen bonds. A spark will excite the molecules so that collisions between them are energetic enough to start the reaction. Once started, the highly exothermic reaction generates enough heat to perpetuate itself. The activation energy can be thought of as a hump that the reactants must cross before the reaction can begin, as illustrated in Figure 6.2.

The next chapter will explore the product of chemical reactions, the bonds that form between atoms.

Chemical Bonds

Atoms in a molecule are joined by bonds. Bonds are formed when the valence or outermost electrons of two or more atoms interact. The nature of the bond between atoms goes a long way toward determining the properties of the molecule. Chapter 5 introduced the two common types of chemical bonds: covalent and ionic. Elements with similar electronegativities share electrons and form covalent bonds. But elements with greatly different electronegativities exchange one or more electrons. This is called an ionic bond.

IONIC BONDS

When atoms exchange or share electrons, they do so to reach a more stable state. The most stable state of an atom is reached when all of its electron shells are filled—like our old friends the noble gases. Table 4.1 in Chapter 4 gave the electron configurations of the noble gases. Each one has eight electrons in its outermost orbital. This realization led chemists to the octet rule, which states that elements tend to lose, gain, or share electrons to achieve an outer principal energy shell with eight electrons. There are exceptions to the octet rule. Hydrogen and lithium, for instance, require only two electrons to fill their outer orbital. But the octet rule works well for most elements.

Atoms go about getting eight valence electrons in the least energetic fashion. Sodium has the following electron configuration:

$$\text{Na } (Z = 11) \; 1s^2 \; 2s^2 \; 2p^6 \; 3s^1$$

The lowest-energy path for sodium to get eight electrons in its outer energy shell is to lose the electron in the 3s orbital. This creates an ion with a net charge of +1, which is written as Na^+. All of the Group 1 alkali metals behave the same way, readily losing electrons in chemical reactions to form positively charged ions. Because positively charged ions migrate to a negatively charged cathode, they are called **cations**.

The alkaline earth metals in Group 2 of the periodic table must lose two electrons to reach a more stable state. Magnesium is an alkaline earth metal with an electron configuration of

$$\text{Mg } (Z = 12) \; 1s^2 \; 2s^2 \; 2p^6 \; 3s^2$$

It must lose two electrons in its 3s orbital to obey the octet rule. This creates a magnesium ion with a charge of +2. Thus, a magnesium ion has the same electron configuration as the sodium ion but a different charge. Both ions have the same stable electron configuration as the noble gas neon:

$$\text{Ne } (Z = 10) \; 1s^2 \; 2s^2 \; 2p^6$$
$$\text{Na}^+ \; (Z = 11) \; 1s^2 \; 2s^2 \; 2p^6$$
$$\text{Mg}^{++} \; (Z = 12) \; 1s^2 \; 2s^2 \; 2p^6$$

Cation formation gets trickier for atoms with higher atomic numbers. Cadmium, for instance, lies between the noble gases krypton and xenon:

$$Kr\ (Z = 36)\ [Ar]3d^{10}\ 4s^2\ 4p^6$$
$$Cd\ (Z = 48)\ [Ar]3d^{10}\ 4s^2\ 4p^6\ 5s^2\ 4d^{10}$$
$$Xe\ (Z = 54)\ [Ar]3d^{10}\ 4s^2\ 4p^6\ 4d^{10}\ 5s^2\ 5p^6$$

Cadmium would have to lose 12 electrons to reach the electron configuration of krypton. It would have to gain six electrons to achieve the configuration of xenon. To reach either configuration would result in cadmium ions with outlandishly high charges. To create such ions would require an enormous amount of energy. So what does cadmium do in a chemical reaction with an electron acceptor? It cannot get to a noble gas configuration, but it does have a filled electron shell, $n = 4$. In a chemical reaction with an electron acceptor, cadmium gives up the two electrons in the $5s$ orbital, leaving a filled outer energy shell:

$$Cd[Ar]3d^{10}\ 4s^2\ 4p^6\ 5s^2\ 4d^{10} \rightarrow Cd^{++}[Ar]3d^{10}\ 4s^2\ 4p^6$$
$$4d^{10}\ +\ 2e^-$$

Figure 5.3 showed that the trend of ionization energies increases as one goes from left to right in the periodic table. On the far right, next to the noble gases, are the halogens. Chlorine is typical of the group.

Chlorine would have to lose seven electrons to reach an electron configuration like that of neon. But if it gained one, it would have the same stable electron configuration as argon. So that is what chlorine does. If it meets an atom with a high-energy valence electron, such as sodium, the electron migrates to the chlorine atom and forms a chloride ion:

$$Cl[Ne]3s^2\ 3p^5\ +\ e^- \rightarrow Cl^-[Ne]3s^2\ 3p^6$$

When sodium reacts with chlorine to form NaCl, an electron moves from a sodium atom to a chlorine atom. The result is a compound composed of sodium ions and chloride ions, Na^+Cl^-, held together by an ionic bond. Ionic bonds do not hold molecules together by sharing electrons; they hold them together because of the electrostatic attraction between the two oppositely charged ions.

COVALENT BONDS

Covalent bonds form between atoms with similar electronegativities. In these reactions, electrons do not migrate from one atom to another as they do in ionic bonds; they are shared by the atoms in the molecule. A good way to visualize this was proposed by Gilbert Lewis, a chemist at the University of California, Berkeley. His representations of molecular bonds are called Lewis dot structures. These structures use dots to denote the valence electrons of an element or molecule.

Lewis structures were conceived in the early twentieth century when chemists still believed that electrons were tiny objects whirling around a nucleus. That picture is now outmoded, but Lewis structures are still helpful in visualizing and understanding chemical reactions.

The Lewis dot structures for hydrogen, oxygen, and water are

$$2\ H\odot + \ \overset{\displaystyle ..}{\underset{\displaystyle ..}{:O}} \ \longrightarrow \ \overset{\displaystyle ..}{\underset{\displaystyle \underset{H}{\odot_\bullet}}{:O}} H$$

• Oxygen electron
⊙ Hydrogen electron

The shared electrons in the water molecule fill the outer energy shell of both hydrogen and oxygen. The electron configuration of the molecule, including the two shared electrons, is shown in Figure 7.1.

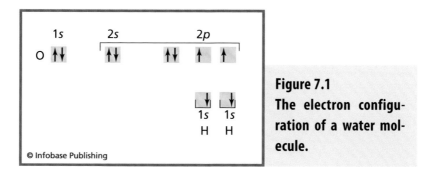

Figure 7.1
The electron configuration of a water molecule.

The difference in electronegativity between sodium and chlorine and between hydrogen and oxygen causes one pair of atoms to form an ionic bond and the other pair to form a covalent bond.

The electronegativity of sodium and chlorine differ by 2.23, whereas the difference between hydrogen and oxygen is only 1.24 (see Table 7.1). As a general rule, molecules made up of two atoms with electronegativity differences greater than 2.0 form ionic bonds. Molecules whose atoms have electronegativity differences of less than 2.0 form covalent bonds. Ionic-bonded salt and covalent-bonded water conform to that rule.

If two atoms have the same electronegativity, then the bond between them is purely covalent. Hydrogen, for instance, occurs as two joined atoms, H-H. Since both atoms in the molecule have the same electronegativity, they form a pure covalent bond with two electrons shared equally by the atoms.

TABLE 7.1 PAULING SCALE	
ELEMENT	ELECTRONEGATIVITY
Sodium	0.93
Chlorine	3.16
Hydrogen	2.20
Oxygen	3.44

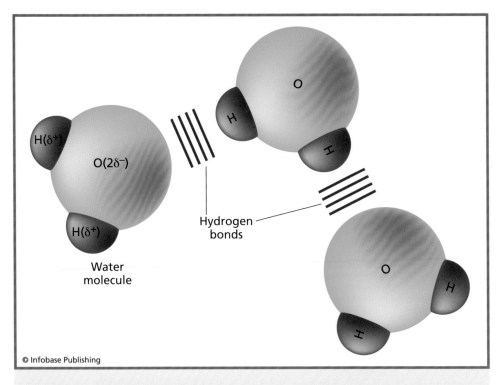

Figure 7.2 Hydrogen bonds form between the slightly positive hydrogen atoms and the slightly negative oxygen atoms of water molecules.

Water, on the other hand, is composed of different atoms. Oxygen is considerably more electronegative than hydrogen, but not so different as to completely capture hydrogen's electron. Nevertheless, the higher electronegativity of oxygen pulls the electron to it more strongly than hydrogen does. Covalent bonds such as this have some ionic character. In the case of water, that means that the oxygen atom has a small negative charge and the hydrogen atoms are slightly positive. This separation of charges creates an **electric dipole**, and the bonds that create the slight separation of charges are called **polar covalent bonds**.

One important result of polar covalent bonding in some molecules is to encourage **hydrogen bonds** to form between molecules. A hydrogen bond is an electrostatic interaction between the highly electronegative elements in a molecule—such as fluorine, chlorine, or oxygen—and the slightly positive hydrogen atoms in a neighboring molecule. Hydrogen bonds are bonds between molecules. They are much weaker than the ionic or covalent bonds that hold molecules together. Still, hydrogen bonds can have a big effect on the nature of a substance. Water is a good example of hydrogen bonding. Because of their small positive charge, the hydrogen atoms tend to associate with the oxygen atoms in nearby molecules as shown in Figure 7.2.

Because of the electric interaction, hydrogen-bonded molecules hold on to each other more tightly than those in substances with pure covalent bonds. This cohesiveness is why water is a liquid at room temperature, whereas heavier covalent-bonded molecules such as chlorine, in the form of Cl_2, are gases.

The cohesiveness of water also contributes to its high **surface tension**. The electrostatic attraction between molecules at the surface causes them to cling to one another and to the molecules below them. The result is a surface that behaves as though it had a thin membrane stretched over it. Visit a pond on a summer day. A careful observer will likely see a large bug walking on the surface of the pond. The bug is a water strider, and it depends on the high surface tension created by hydrogen bonds in the water to keep it from sinking.

Some molecules held together by polar covalent bonds are not polar themselves. The symmetry of these molecules cancels the separation of the charges between the individual atoms that creates the polarity. Carbon tetrachloride, CCl_4, is a good example.

- Chlorine electron
- Carbon electron

(continues on page 90)

THE MOST IMPORTANT HYDROGEN BOND

One DNA strand introduces itself to another strand, "The name is Bond. Hydrogen Bond. Let's connect." It is an old joke but an appropriate one. Hydrogen bonding plays a critical role in the structure of deoxyribonucleic acid (DNA), the carrier of the genetic code and the molecule that is essential for all life on Earth.

The crucial constituents of DNA are four bases that scientists abbreviate as A, C, G, and T. If you uncoiled all the DNA in the nucleus of a single cell, it would form a 6-foot-long string upon which those four letters are repeated in various combinations about 3 billion times. The order of the letters is the genetic code.

All multicellular life starts as a single cell. Copies of the DNA in that cell must eventually occupy almost every one of the trillions of cells in a human body. For that to happen, the DNA in the original cell must replicate itself many times. The key to this replication is the famous double helix. When two strands of DNA— let's call them X and Y—separate, each strand can assemble the other. X builds a new Y, forming a fresh double helix. Y does the same thing. This doubles the number of DNA molecules. This mechanism depends on the two strands of DNA being able to hold together under normal conditions, yet unwind easily. That is where hydrogen bonds come in.

Each of the two strands of the double helix consists of a backbone of sugars and phosphates held together by strong covalent bonds. Attached to the strands are the bases. The bases contain highly electronegative nitrogen and oxygen atoms with hydrogen atoms attached to them. The strongly electronegative atoms on one strand share a hydrogen with an electronegative atom on the other strand, forming a hydrogen bond. Two hydrogen bonds hold an A to a T. Three of them bind C to G, as shown in the figure. The double helix that Francis Crick—the Nobel Prize winner and co-discoverer (with James Watson) of the structure of DNA—famously labeled "the secret of life"[6] depends on the weak hydrogen bond for its most important property.

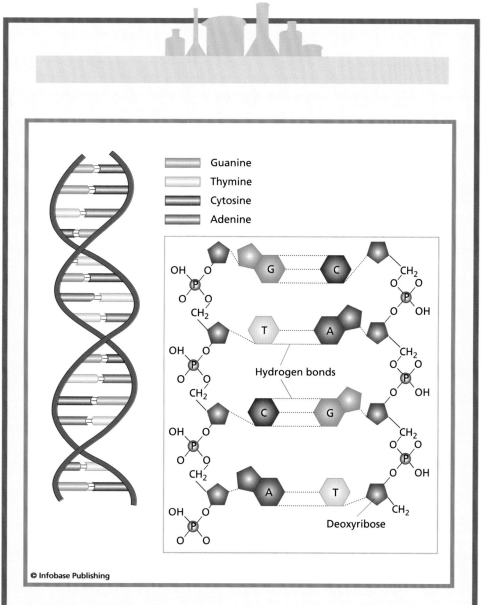

Guanine
Thymine
Cytosine
Adenine

© Infobase Publishing

The structure of DNA resembles a ladder that has been twisted around itself. The rungs of the ladder are composed of bases (guanine, thymine, cytosine, and adenine) that form hydrogen bonds.

(continued from page 87)

Chlorine is much more electronegative than carbon, so a strong electric dipole exists between each chlorine and the carbon atom. The chlorine atoms are symmetrically arranged around the carbon so that the molecule itself is not polar, even though it has four polar covalent bonds between its atoms.

The next section will explore other types of covalent bonds.

DOUBLE BONDS, TRIPLE BONDS, AND RESONANCE

The more complex molecules examined here require a better way to specify their structure. A simple example is water, represented by the **molecular formula** H_2O. This shows a chemist that there are two atoms of hydrogen and one of oxygen in this molecule. It does not indicate how the atoms are arranged. Throughout this book, the structure of water has been assumed to be HOH, with the two hydrogen atoms attached to the oxygen. But based solely on the molecular formula, H_2O could have a different structure, HHO, with a bond between the two hydrogen atoms and another between one of the hydrogen atoms and the oxygen. Lewis dot structures show how a molecule is put together, but with big, complicated molecules, drawing Lewis structures is not practical.

Modern **structural formulas** use a dash to indicate a covalent bond made up of a pair of electrons, one from each atom. The structural formula for water is H—O—H. The structural formulas for a few other common substances are shown in Figure 7.3.

To reach the lower energy state of a filled energy shell, atoms sometimes share more than one electron. Oxygen, for example, has an outer p orbital with six electrons. The most common form of oxygen is O_2. To complete the electron shells of both atoms, they must share two electrons. The reaction to form the molecule and its structure would then be represented as:

$$:\overset{..}{\underset{..}{O}}: \; + \; :\overset{..}{\underset{..}{O}}: \; \longrightarrow \; :\overset{..}{\underset{..}{O}}::\overset{..}{\underset{..}{O}}: \quad \text{or} \quad O + O \longrightarrow O = O$$

In the structural formula for O_2, the sharing of two pairs of electrons is represented by two parallel dashes—a **double bond**. Sometimes three pairs of electrons are shared, producing a **triple bond**, which is indicated by three parallel dashes.

N_2	C_2H_2	HCN
N≡N	H – C≡C – H	H – C≡N
Nitrogen	Acetylene	Hydrogen cyanide

Sometimes there is more than one correct structural formula for a compound with double or triple bonds. Ozone, for example, can be correctly written as one of two forms.

Ozone

Another example is benzene, a cyclical **aromatic compound**.

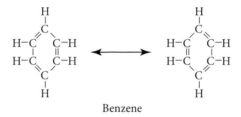
Benzene

Which of two formulas for benzene is correct? The answer is neither. The two forms are called **resonance** structures. The term "resonance" is a bit misleading because it implies that the two forms are oscillating back and forth. In reality, the carbon-carbon bond lengths in a resonating structure such as benzene are all the same. Resonant structures have only one form, a resonance hybrid somewhere between the two possibilities.

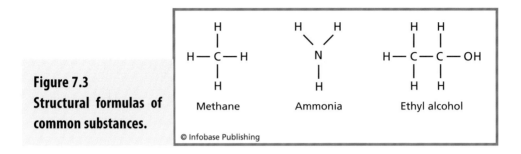

Figure 7.3
Structural formulas of common substances.

© Infobase Publishing

Resonance structures result from a phenomenon known as **electron delocalization**. The electron pairs in the three double bonds in a benzene ring are delocalized. These are electrons that belong to no particular atom or bond. As a consequence, no ordinary double bonds exist in a benzene ring. The electrons are in an orbital that extends across adjacent atoms. This smear of electrons is usually represented as a circle within the ring.

Resonant forms of molecules are more stable than the structures from which they form. The new orbitals extend over the entire molecule. This allows the electrons to have longer wavelengths and correspondingly lower energy. Delocalization also plays a role in the last two topics covered in this chapter: **molecular orbitals** and **metallic bonding**.

MOLECULAR ORBITALS

The structural formulas used to represent molecules are based on valence bond theory. Double and triple bonds are just additional pairs of shared valence electrons. But structural formulas—while useful—do not tell the whole story about the nature of the bonds between atoms in a molecule. Valence bond theory falls flat when it tries to explain delocalized electrons and resonating structures. To get at what is really going on inside a molecule, chemists had to dig deeper.

The Lewis dot structure and the molecular formula for the simplest molecule, H_2, are

$$H - H \qquad H \vdots H$$

What does that mean in terms of the orbitals of the atoms? What actually happens when the clouds of valence electrons of atoms merge to form a molecule? The answer is that the molecule develops its own orbitals, called molecular orbitals, which can be described as a combination of the valence orbitals of the atoms in the molecule.

To get the molecular orbital of the hydrogen molecule, the orbital equations of the two atoms are combined. When the orbital equations are added together, the result is a bonding molecular orbital that extends over both atoms. Subtracting the orbital equations of the atoms produces an antibonding molecular orbital. This process is called the linear combination of atomic orbitals or LCAO.

When two hydrogen atoms come together, the two spherical *s* orbitals interact to form a dumbbell-shaped molecular orbital. When that orbital is occupied by two electrons, it is called a sigma bond, as shown in Figure 7.4. It is called a sigma bond because the molecular orbital appears spherical—like an s orbital—when viewed along the bonding axis. (*Sigma* is the English word for the Greek letter σ, which corresponds to the English letter *s*.)

The bonding orbital in a hydrogen molecule has a high electron density between the two positively charged nuclei. This mediates

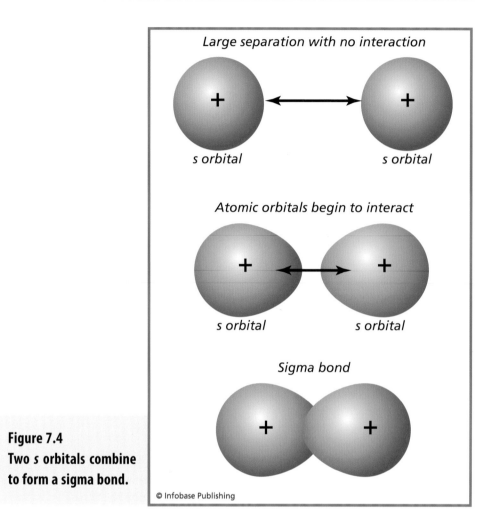

Figure 7.4
Two s orbitals combine to form a sigma bond.

the repulsion between the nuclei and gives the molecule a lower energy than that of the reacting atoms. Energy must be added to break the hydrogen atoms apart. The antibonding orbital, however, has a low electron density between the nuclei, making it a more energetic structure than either of the individual atoms or the bonded molecule. This is illustrated graphically in Figure 7.5.

Atoms with p orbitals can also form sigma bonds. Fluorine $(1s^2\ 2s^2\ 2p^{5)}$ has a half-filled p orbital. When it reacts with another

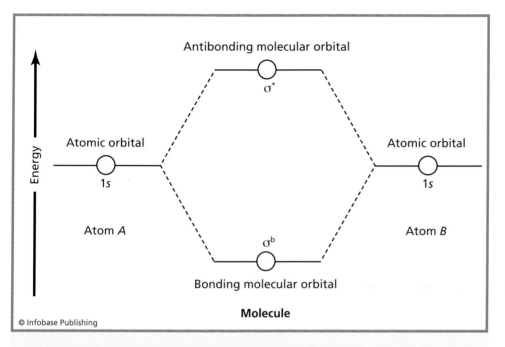

Figure 7.5   Bonding and antibonding molecular orbitals for the H₂ molecule. Antibonding orbitals are higher energy orbitals than bonding orbitals.

fluorine atom the two *p* orbitals overlap end-to-end to form a bond that is symmetrical along the bonding axis (Figure 7.6).

When two *p* orbitals overlap in a side-by-side configuration, they form a pi bond, shown in Figure 7.7. This bond is named after the Greek letter π. The electron clouds in pi bonds overlap less than those in sigma bonds, and they are correspondingly weaker. Pi bonds are often found in molecules with double or triple bonds. One example is ethene, commonly known as ethylene, a simple double-bonded molecule (Figure 7.8). The two vertical *p* orbitals form a pi bond. The two horizontal orbitals form a sigma bond.

Molecular orbital theory explains much about molecules. It can tell a chemist how far apart the atoms are, the bonding angles between them, and the energy of the electrons. But molecular orbital theory

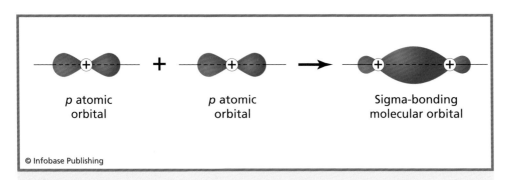

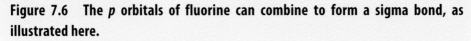

© Infobase Publishing

Figure 7.6 **The *p* orbitals of fluorine can combine to form a sigma bond, as illustrated here.**

requires the manipulation of complicated wave functions, a cumbersome process. Two easier, but less rigorous, methods for getting at the arrangements of atoms in a molecule have been developed.

Hybridized Orbital Method

The **hybridized orbital** approach is a simplified way of predicting the geometry of a molecule by mixing the valence orbitals of its atoms. For example, methane (CH_4) is composed of a carbon atom with an electron configuration of $1s^2\ 2s^2\ 2p^2$. The hydrogen atom has an electron configuration of $1s$. The geometry of the methane

Figure 7.7

When *p* orbitals overlap in a side-by-side configuration, they form a pi bond.

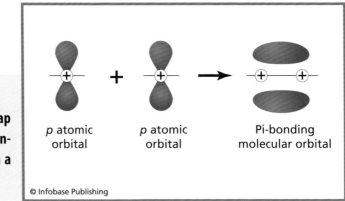

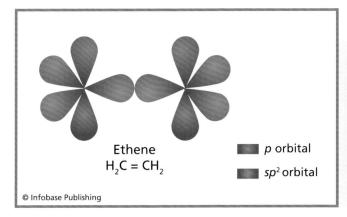

Ethene
$H_2C = CH_2$

■ *p* orbital
■ *sp²* orbital

© Infobase Publishing

Figure 7.8 **The double bond of ethene (C_2H_4). The vertical *p* orbitals of ethene form a pi bond, while the horizontal *sp²* orbitals form a sigma bond.**

molecule is known to be tetrahedral, with all of the carbon-hydrogen bond distances being equal. Chemists needed a simpler way than the complete molecular orbital treatment to answer this question: How can hydrogen combine with carbon's *s* and *p* orbitals, which are quite different in shape and length, to produce a molecule with four equal bond lengths?

To explain this and the geometry of other molecules, the chemist Linus Pauling suggested in 1931 that the atomic orbitals of carbon

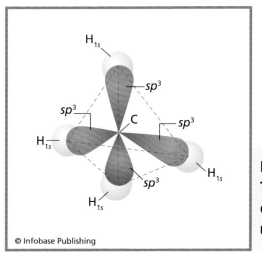

© Infobase Publishing

Figure 7.9 Tetrahedral structure of the methane (CH_4) molecule.

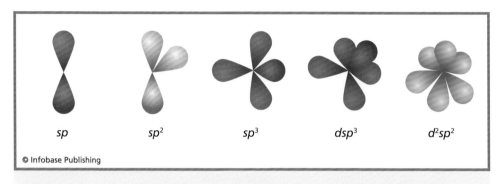

Figure 7.10   Different types of hybridization and the resulting orbital shapes.

(and other atoms) hybridize during reaction. Instead of its *s* orbitals and *p* orbitals interacting with hydrogen, carbon forms four identical hybrid orbitals called *sp*³ orbitals. These orbitals combine with the hydrogen atoms to form sigma bonds. The result is the tetrahedral structure shown in Figure 7.9, with all bond lengths the same. The hybridized structure fit the experimental data nicely. Since then, the concept of hybridization has been extended to other atomic orbitals. The shapes of many of them are shown in Figure 7.10.

VSEPR Theory

The other approach to molecular geometry is the **valence shell electron-pair repulsion (VSEPR)** theory. This theory holds that the shapes of molecules are determined by the repulsion between electron pairs around a central atom. This would explain why the bonding angle in water is not 90°. One would expect a 90° angle if hydrogen formed two sigma bonds with the *p* orbitals of oxygen, which are at right angles to one another. The actual angle of 105° is better explained by the repulsion between the valence electron pairs. The repulsion produces a tetrahedral structure for water, with two positions occupied by hydrogen atoms and the other two by unbonded electron pairs.

VSEPR theory works best when predicting the shapes of molecules composed of a central atom surrounded by bonded atoms and nonbonding electrons. Some of the possible shapes of molecules that contain a central atom are given in Figure 7.11, along with the chemical formulas of molecules that have that shape.

METALLIC BONDS

This is the last bond type to be considered. Let's start with a question: What holds a metal together? A bar of copper or magnesium has properties that are entirely different from substances held together by ionic or covalent bonds. Metals are dense structures that conduct electricity readily. They are malleable, which means that they can be easily twisted into shapes. They are ductile, which allows them to be drawn into wires. No substances with ionic or covalent bonds, such as salt or water, behave anything like metals.

One clue to understanding the nature of metallic bonds comes from their high electrical conductivity. Like most substances held together by ionic or covalent bonds, pure water and pure salt do not conduct electricity well. But pure copper does. Electrical conductivity is a measure of how free the electrons are to move. The high conductivity of metals indicates that their electrons are freer to move than the electrons are in salt or water.

The freedom of electrons to move easily, coupled with the metals' high density, led scientists to hypothesize that they were densely packed lattices of positively charged atoms immersed in a sea of freely moving valence electrons. This structure, illustrated in Figure 7.12, is accepted today.

The concept of electrons not "belonging" to any particular atom in a molecule brings us back to resonance structures. The electrons in a metal are also delocalized. An electron in a bar of sodium is not associated with any particular atom, just as the electrons in the double bonds of benzene are not associated with any particular atom.

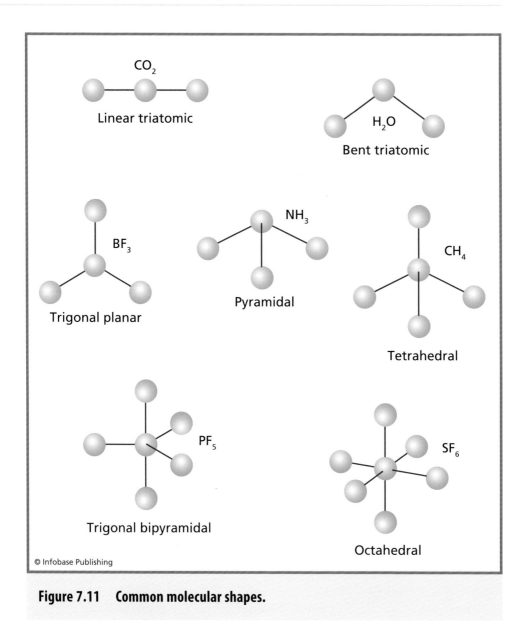

Figure 7.11   Common molecular shapes.

Each atom in a bar of sodium has the same outer $3s$ orbital containing one electron. The individual atomic orbitals overlap, creating a huge number of molecular orbitals among which the electrons can move freely. This gives sodium and the other metals

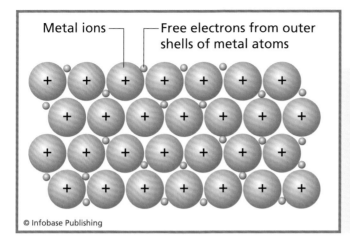

Metal ions ——— ┌—Free electrons from outer
shells of metal atoms

© Infobase Publishing

**Figure 7.12
The outer electrons of
metals are not bound
to any one atom and
easily move around in
a sea of freely moving
electrons.**

their high electric conductivity. Pump in an electron at one end of
a metal wire, and an electron from an almost identical orbital pops
out at the other end. The delocalized electrons of the metallic bond
ensure that little energy is lost in this process, making metal wires
the preferred material in power lines.

Common
Compounds,
Uncommon Results

This chapter will explore how chemists have used their hard-won knowledge of atoms and molecules to better understand the day-to-day world around us. Salt and water are two of the more common and most important compounds on Earth. What properties make them important? What aspect of their chemistry gives them those properties?

Sodium chloride is a white, crystalline substance held together by the electrostatic forces between its two constituents, sodium ions and chloride ions. Salt is essential for human life. An average person has almost a quarter pound of it distributed throughout his or her body. Many of the sodium ions are found in the blood, where, among other things, they regulate blood pressure. Because salt is lost in sweat and urine, a normal diet requires us to consume it regularly.

Salt has been important to humans for as long as our species has been around, but it became more important after the development of agriculture. Meat contains salt, but vegetables do not have enough to sustain us. Deer must have **salt licks** to get enough salt; wolves do not need them.

SALT AND WATER

Salt has been important to our species in other ways, too. Next to keeping us alive and making our food taste better, probably the oldest and most important use of salt was in the preservation of meat and fish. In the days before refrigeration, salt was used extensively as a preservative. Even if meat was to be smoked or dried, it was often soaked in brine (saltwater) beforehand. Salting was the only method for preserving fish that worked well on a fishing vessel at sea. It was either catch a few fish and return to port to deliver them before they spoiled, or preserve the catch by salting on the ship and stay at sea longer. Salting enabled European fishermen to travel long distances and exploit one of the most productive fisheries in the world: the great cod fishing grounds of the North Atlantic. Ships left ports in Europe filled with salt and returned filled with salted cod.

The preservative powers of salt stem from its chemistry and its interaction with water. The H_2O molecule is a tetrahedral structure. It does not look like a tetrahedron because two of the positions are occupied not by atoms but by electron pairs. Another molecule with a tetrahedral structure is carbon tetrachloride. The difference between the structures of the two molecules is that carbon tetrachloride has no unbonded electron pairs (Figure 8.1).

Because chlorine is more electronegative than carbon, carbon tetrachloride has four polar covalent bonds. But, as pointed out earlier, the molecular symmetry cancels out the electric dipoles of the individual bonds. The result is a nonpolar molecule. Like water, carbon tetrachloride is a good solvent. At one time, it was used as a dry cleaning agent. Water and carbon tetrachloride, however, dissolve entirely different classes of compounds. Carbon tetrachloride forms solutions with nonpolar organic compounds. It is infinitely **miscible**, for example, with benzene, whereas water and benzene do not mix.

Figure 8.1
Both water and carbon tetrachloride (CCl₄) are tetrahedral structures. Unlike water, carbon tetrachloride does not have any unbonded electron pairs.

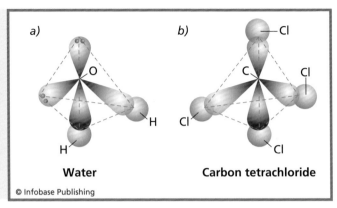

Water   Carbon tetrachloride

© Infobase Publishing

Water, however, is a wonderful solvent for ionic-bonded substances such as salt. The secret to its success lies in the electric dipoles created by the polar covalent bonds between the hydrogen and oxygen atoms. In water, the polar bonds are asymmetric. The hydrogen side is positive; the oxygen side is negative. One measure of the amount of charge separation in a molecule is its **dielectric constant**. Water has a dielectric constant that is considerably higher than that of any other common liquid.

A crystal of salt is a lattice, an alternating arrangement of positively charged sodium ions and negatively charged chloride ions. When water is added to the crystal, the positive ends of the water molecules associate with negative chloride ions and the negative ends link up with the sodium ions. In effect, the water molecules pry the two ions apart. Once in solution, the water molecules surround the ions. The negatively charged ends of the water molecule face the sodium ions and vice versa for the chloride ions, as shown in Figure 8.2.

Because of the attraction between salt ions and the electric dipoles of water molecules, salt is **hydrophilic**—it attracts water. That brings us back to fish. When cod (or other fish or meats) are packed in

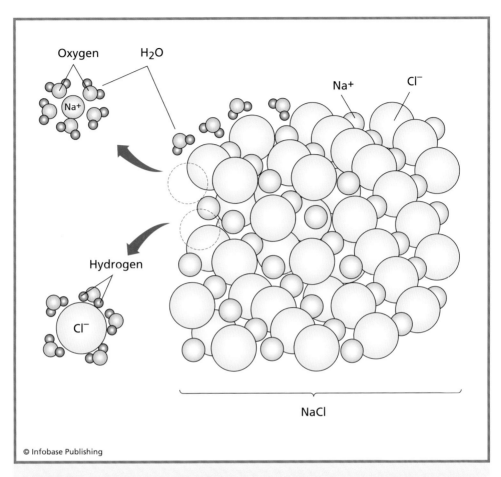

Figure 8.2   Salt consists of positively charged sodium ions and negatively charged chloride ions. When salt dissolves in water, the sodium and chlorine ions are pried apart by water molecules. The slightly positive hydrogen atoms of water surround the chloride ions, while the slightly negative oxygen atoms of water surround the sodium ions.

salt, the salt pulls water from the surrounding flesh and from the bacterial cells, killing or slowing the growth of unwanted bacteria, thus preserving the fish. So effective was salt as a preservative that a thousand years ago Basque fishermen caught and salted cod in the North Atlantic and sold them far to the south. According to Mark Kurlansky's book *Salt: A World History*, "air-dried and salt-cured salt cod, stiff as planks of wood, could be stacked in wagons and hauled over roads, even in warm Mediterranean climates." Although they did not know and might not have cared, the fishermen, the wagoners, and the eventual consumers of salted cod were the unknowing beneficiaries of some unusual chemistry: the interaction of ionic bonded sodium chloride with the highly polar covalent bonds of water.

Salted fish is less common today. Refrigeration has replaced salting as the most convenient way to preserve meat. But in the freezer next to the refrigerated fish, water exhibits yet another uncommon feature—it becomes ice in a most peculiar way.

SALT LICKS

Naturally occurring salt is known as halite. Halite is what's left when seas evaporate. Michigan, for instance, was underwater several times hundreds of millions of years ago. When the seas disappeared, huge deposits of halite were left. At one time or another, seas covered all of the planet, so halite deposits can be found almost anywhere.

Many of these deposits are underground and must be mined to get the salt, but some are on the surface. These are called salt licks, because deer, buffalo, and other animals licked the salt. Without supplemental salt from licks or brine, many herbivorous animals could not survive. A diet of grass and other plants does not provide enough salt to keep them alive. Consequently, animals visit salt licks regularly. The paths they made are the same ones that the early settlers followed, so many of today's cities are located near old salt licks. One path to a salt lick was created by buffalo herds. For that reason, the town that grew up around the lick is now called Buffalo, New York.

These days, salt licks are for sale everywhere. Some are artificial with added ingredients that contribute to "the horse's well-being."[7] Others are natural blocks of salt taken from mines and marketed primarily to deer hunters who want to attract deer to a spot where the hunter will be waiting. Apparently salt licks do their job well. As one advertisement trumpets, "The Bucks Stop Here."[8]

Most liquids—benzene is a good example—behave predictably as the temperature changes. Benzene is a liquid between 5.5°C and 80.1°C, not too different from water, which freezes at 0°C and boils at 100°C. As liquid benzene cools, it becomes more dense. That is expected. As the thermal energy of the molecules decreases, they pack together more tightly. At the freezing point, solid benzene forms. The molecules assume the closest possible packing. This is why the solid phase of most compounds is denser than the liquid phase.

If water acted like benzene, lakes would freeze from the bottom up and become solid ice. In a benzene world, fish could not survive in colder climates. Icebergs would be at the bottom of the sea, and the *Titanic* might still be afloat. The world as we know it would be topsy-turvy if water behaved like benzene. That leads to the question: Why doesn't it?

The answer lies again in water's strongly polar covalent bonds, which enable it to form hydrogen bonds with adjacent molecules. The previous chapter showed how hydrogen bonds hold DNA's double helix together, but hydrogen bonds also form between water molecules. As water cools toward the freezing point, the thermal energy of the molecules decreases and its density increases, just like benzene. At 4°C, something unusual happens: The density of water begins to decrease. Chemists now know that this is because of the association between water molecules due to hydrogen bonding. A partially ordered structure is forming in the cooled water. This partial ordering becomes a rigid lattice in ice. Each water molecule in a crystal of ice is hydrogen bonded to four other molecules (Figure 8.3).

In the hydrogen-bonded lattice of ice, the individual water molecules cannot pack together as tightly as they would if there was no hydrogen bonding. Consequently, the density of ice is lower than that of water. Ice cubes float; benzene cubes sink.

The nature of the bonds between an oxygen atom and two atoms of hydrogen has an enormous impact on how our planet works. Because of the highly polar covalent bond, salt dissolves in water, which enabled our ancestors to preserve meat. It also produces the hydrogen bonds that make our lakes freeze from the top down, per-

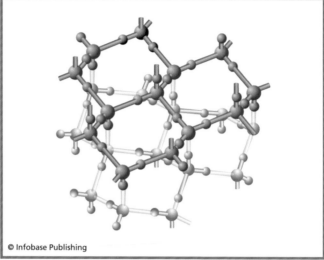

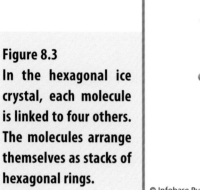

Figure 8.3
In the hexagonal ice crystal, each molecule is linked to four others. The molecules arrange themselves as stacks of hexagonal rings.

mitting ice skaters to enjoy the surface while fish swim below. Finally, hydrogen bonds hold together the strands of our DNA, without which life could not exist.

BEYOND SALT AND WATER

Salt and water are crucial to life on Earth, but many other chemicals are also important. Chemical compounds, both man-made and naturally occurring, number in the millions. They are used in every facet of our lives, from medicine to clothing to food.

One of the first and most useful medicinal chemicals is aspirin ($C_9H_8O_4$), also known as acetylsalicylic acid. This painkiller was first trademarked and manufactured in 1899, but a precursor to the drug had been extracted from the bark of willow trees by Hippocrates as early as the 5th century B.C. The pharmaceutical industry has since developed an array of products to alleviate aches and pains, yet aspirin is still prominent on the shelves of drugstores. In pharmacies that dispense prescription drugs, an even wider array of chemicals is sold to help those with diseases ranging from high blood pressure to cancer.

Your clothing owes its appearance to compounds developed by chemists. The first commercial synthetic dye was produced in the middle of the nineteenth century. It was the purple dye known as mauve ($C_{26}H_{23}N_4$). Naturally occurring chemicals had long been used to color clothing, but they were expensive compared to the synthetic dye. Mauve added color to the clothing of the working classes, rescuing them from the dinginess of plain cotton and wool. Later, chemists developed synthetic fibers. Today, not only does the color of your clothing come from compounds made by chemists, but the fabric itself might have been invented by them.

One of the most important advances in human history came when chemists and engineers figured out how to manufacture fertilizer from the nitrogen in the air. Before that, farmers relied on guano from South America to fertilize their crops. By the beginning of the twentieth century, supplies were running low. The Haber process (named for the German chemist Fritz Haber) for producing ammonia (NH_3) for fertilizer saved the day, enabling the world population to quadruple in the twentieth century. Without synthetic fertilizers made by Haber's process, millions of people would have starved and would be starving today.

All compounds, from the simple ones such as water and ammonia to the most complex, are held together by chemical bonds. All chemical bonds—from purely covalent to strongly ionic—act the way they do because of the nature of the atoms that form the bonds. Our knowledge of those atoms is at the heart of the science of chemistry. Understanding Richard Feynman's "little particles" has enabled mankind to manage the natural world to suit its needs. Feynman was undoubtedly correct when he said that the "atomic hypothesis (or the atomic fact, or whatever you wish to call it)" is the most concise and important summary of scientific knowledge produced by mankind. And it is crucial that every generation passes it on to the next.

PERIODIC TABLE OF THE ELEMENTS

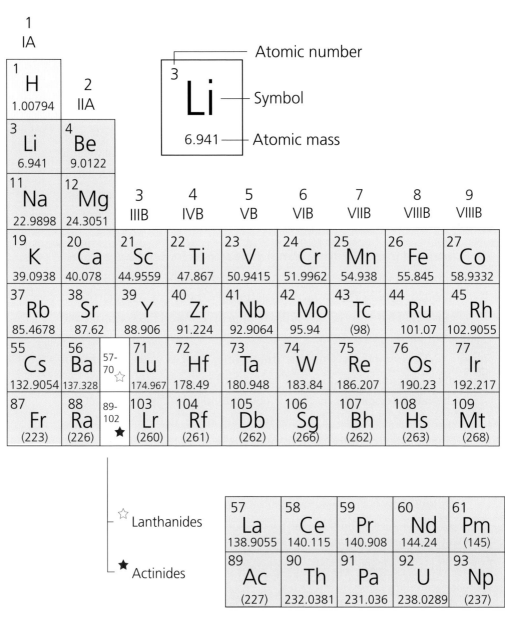

1 IA									
1 **H** 1.00794	**2** IIA								
3 **Li** 6.941	**4** **Be** 9.0122	**3** IIIB	**4** IVB	**5** VB	**6** VIB	**7** VIIB	**8** VIIIB	**9** VIIIB	
11 **Na** 22.9898	**12** **Mg** 24.3051								
19 **K** 39.0938	**20** **Ca** 40.078	**21** **Sc** 44.9559	**22** **Ti** 47.867	**23** **V** 50.9415	**24** **Cr** 51.9962	**25** **Mn** 54.938	**26** **Fe** 55.845	**27** **Co** 58.9332	
37 **Rb** 85.4678	**38** **Sr** 87.62	**39** **Y** 88.906	**40** **Zr** 91.224	**41** **Nb** 92.9064	**42** **Mo** 95.94	**43** **Tc** (98)	**44** **Ru** 101.07	**45** **Rh** 102.9055	
55 **Cs** 132.9054	**56** **Ba** 137.328	57-70 ☆	**71** **Lu** 174.967	**72** **Hf** 178.49	**73** **Ta** 180.948	**74** **W** 183.84	**75** **Re** 186.207	**76** **Os** 190.23	**77** **Ir** 192.217
87 **Fr** (223)	**88** **Ra** (226)	89-102 ★	**103** **Lr** (260)	**104** **Rf** (261)	**105** **Db** (262)	**106** **Sg** (266)	**107** **Bh** (262)	**108** **Hs** (263)	**109** **Mt** (268)

Atomic number

3
Li — Symbol

6.941 — Atomic mass

☆ Lanthanides

★ Actinides

57 **La** 138.9055	**58** **Ce** 140.115	**59** **Pr** 140.908	**60** **Nd** 144.24	**61** **Pm** (145)
89 **Ac** (227)	**90** **Th** 232.0381	**91** **Pa** 231.036	**92** **U** 238.0289	**93** **Np** (237)

Numbers in parentheses are atomic mass numbers of most stable isotopes.

Metals

Non-metals

Metalloids

							18 VIIIA
		13 IIIA	14 IVA	15 VA	16 VIA	17 VIIA	2 He 4.0026

13 IIIA	14 IVA	15 VA	16 VIA	17 VIIA	18 VIIIA
5 B 10.81	6 C 12.011	7 N 14.0067	8 O 15.9994	9 F 18.9984	10 Ne 20.1798

10 VIIIB	11 IB	12 IIB	13 Al 26.9815	14 Si 28.0855	15 P 30.9738	16 S 32.067	17 Cl 35.4528	18 Ar 39.948
28 Ni 58.6934	29 Cu 63.546	30 Zn 65.409	31 Ga 69.723	32 Ge 72.61	33 As 74.9216	34 Se 78.96	35 Br 79.904	36 Kr 83.798
46 Pd 106.42	47 Ag 107.8682	48 Cd 112.412	49 In 114.818	50 Sn 118.711	51 Sb 121.760	52 Te 127.60	53 I 126.9045	54 Xe 131.29
78 Pt 195.08	79 Au 196.9655	80 Hg 200.59	81 Tl 204.3833	82 Pb 207.2	83 Bi 208.9804	84 Po (209)	85 At (210)	86 Rn (222)
110 Ds (271)	111 Rg (272)	112 Uub (277)						

62 Sm 150.36	63 Eu 151.966	64 Gd 157.25	65 Tb 158.9253	66 Dy 162.500	67 Ho 164.9303	68 Er 167.26	69 Tm 168.9342	70 Yb 173.04
94 Pu (244)	95 Am 243	96 Cm (247)	97 Bk (247)	98 Cf (251)	99 Es (252)	100 Fm (257)	101 Md (258)	102 No (259)

ELECTRON CONFIGURATIONS

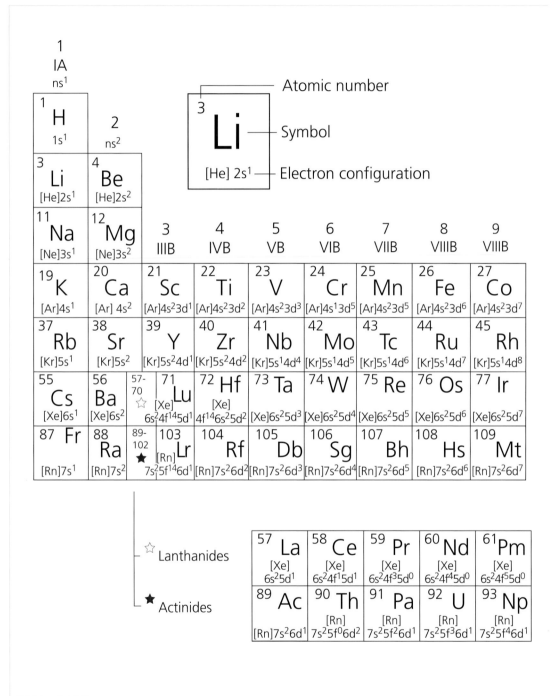

				18 VIIIA ns^2np^6

Top section (groups 13–18):

13 IIIA ns^2np^1	14 IVA ns^2np^2	15 VA ns^2np^3	16 VIA ns^2np^4	17 VIIA ns^2np^5	2 **He** $1s^2$
5 **B** $[He]2s^22p^1$	6 **C** $[He]2s^22p^2$	7 **N** $[He]2s^22p^3$	8 **O** $[He]2s^22p^4$	9 **F** $[He]2s^22p^5$	10 **Ne** $[He]2s^22p^6$
13 **Al** $[Ne]3s^23p^1$	14 **Si** $[Ne]3s^23p^2$	15 **P** $[Ne]3s^23p^3$	16 **S** $[Ne]3s^23p^4$	17 **Cl** $[Ne]3s^23p^5$	18 **Ar** $[Ne]3s^23p^6$

10 VIIIB	11 IB	12 IIB							
28 **Ni** $[Ar]4s^23d^8$	29 **Cu** $[Ar]4s^13d^{10}$	30 **Zn** $[Ar]4s^23d^{10}$	31 **Ga** $[Ar]4s^24p^1$	32 **Ge** $[Ar]4s^24p^2$	33 **As** $[Ar]4s^24p^3$	34 **Se** $[Ar]4s^24p^4$	35 **Br** $[Ar]4s^24p^5$	36 **Kr** $[Ar]4s^24p^6$
46 **Pd** $[Kr]4d^{10}$	47 **Ag** $[Kr]5s^14d^{10}$	48 **Cd** $[Kr]5s^24d^{10}$	49 **In** $[Kr]5s^25p^1$	50 **Sn** $[Kr]5s^25p^2$	51 **Sb** $[Kr]5s^25p^3$	52 **Te** $[Kr]5s^25p^4$	53 **I** $[Kr]5s^25p^5$	54 **Xe** $[Kr]5s^25p^6$
78 **Pt** $[Xe]6s^15d^9$	79 **Au** $[Xe]6s^15d^{10}$	80 **Hg** $[Xe]6s^25d^{10}$	81 **Tl** $[Xe]6s^26p^1$	82 **Pb** $[Xe]6s^26p^2$	83 **Bi** $[Xe]6s^26p^3$	84 **Po** $[Xe]6s^26p^4$	85 **At** $[Xe]6s^26p^5$	86 **Rn** $[Xe]6s^26p^6$
110 **Ds** $[Rn]7s^16d^9$	111 **Rg** $[Rn]7s^16d^{10}$	112 **Uub** $[Rn]7s^26d^{10}$						

62 **Sm** $[Xe]$ $6s^24f^65d^0$	63 **Eu** $[Xe]$ $6s^24f^75d^0$	64 **Gd** $[Xe]$ $6s^24f^75d^1$	65 **Tb** $[Xe]$ $6s^24f^95d^0$	66 **Dy** $[Xe]$ $6s^24f^{10}5d^0$	67 **Ho** $[Xe]$ $6s^24f^{11}5d^0$	68 **Er** $[Xe]$ $6s^24f^{12}5d^0$	69 **Tm** $[Xe]$ $6s^24f^{13}5d^0$	70 **Yb** $[Xe]$ $6s^24f^{14}5d^0$
94 **Pu** $[Rn]$ $7s^25f^66d^0$	95 **Am** $[Rn]$ $7s^25f^76d^0$	96 **Cm** $[Rn]$ $7s^25f^76d^1$	97 **Bk** $[Rn]$ $7s^25f^96d^0$	98 **Cf** $[Rn]$ $7s^25f^{10}6d^0$	99 **Es** $[Rn]$ $7s^25f^{11}6d^0$	100 **Fm** $[Rn]$ $7s^25f^{12}6d^0$	101 **Md** $[Rn]$ $7s^25f^{13}6d^0$	102 **No** $[Rn]$ $7s^25f^{14}6d^1$

TABLE OF ATOMIC MASSES

ELEMENT	SYMBOL	ATOMIC NUMBER	ATOMIC MASS
Actinium	Ac	89	(227)
Aluminum	Al	13	26.9815
Americium	Am	95	243
Antimony	Sb	51	121.76
Argon	Ar	18	39.948
Arsenic	As	33	74.9216
Astatine	At	85	(210)
Barium	Ba	56	137.328
Berkelium	Bk	97	(247)
Beryllium	Be	4	9.0122
Bismuth	Bi	83	208.9804
Bohrium	Bh	107	(262)
Boron	B	5	10.81
Bromine	Br	35	79.904
Cadmium	Cd	48	112.412
Calcium	Ca	20	40.078
Californium	Cf	98	(251)
Carbon	C	6	12.011
Cerium	Ce	58	140.115
Cesium	Cs	55	132.9054
Chlorine	Cl	17	35.4528
Chromium	Cr	24	51.9962
Cobalt	Co	27	58.9332
Copper	Cu	29	63.546
Curium	Cm	96	(247)
Darmstadtium	Ds	110	(271)
Dubnium	Db	105	(262)
Dysprosium	Dy	66	162.5
Einsteinium	Es	99	(252)
Erbium	Er	68	167.26
Europium	Eu	63	151.966
Fermium	Fm	100	(257)
Fluorine	F	9	18.9984

ELEMENT	SYMBOL	ATOMIC NUMBER	ATOMIC MASS
Francium	Fr	87	(223)
Gadolinium	Gd	64	157.25
Gallium	Ga	31	69.723
Germanium	Ge	32	72.61
Gold	Au	79	196.9655
Hafnium	Hf	72	178.49
Hassium	Hs	108	(263)
Helium	He	2	4.0026
Holmium	Ho	67	164.9303
Hydrogen	H	1	1.00794
Indium	In	49	114.818
Iodine	I	53	126.9045
Iridium	Ir	77	192.217
Iron	Fe	26	55.845
Krypton	Kr	36	83.798
Lanthanum	La	57	138.9055
Lawrencium	Lr	103	(260)
Lead	Pb	82	207.2
Lithium	Li	3	6.941
Lutetium	Lu	71	174.967
Magnesium	Mg	12	24.3051
Manganese	Mn	25	54.938
Meitnerium	Mt	109	(268)
Mendelevium	Md	101	(258)
Mercury	Hg	80	200.59
Molybdenum	Mo	42	95.94
Neodymium	Nd	60	144.24
Neon	Ne	10	20.1798
Neptunium	Np	93	(237)
Nickel	Ni	28	58.6934
Niobium	Nb	41	92.9064
Nitrogen	N	7	14.0067
Nobelium	No	102	(259)

ELEMENT	SYMBOL	ATOMIC NUMBER	ATOMIC MASS
Osmium	Os	76	190.23
Oxygen	O	8	15.9994
Palladium	Pd	46	106.42
Phosphorus	P	15	30.9738
Platinum	Pt	78	195.08
Plutonium	Pu	94	(244)
Polonium	Po	84	(209)
Potassium	K	19	39.0938
Praseodymium	Pr	59	140.908
Promethium	Pm	61	(145)
Protactinium	Pa	91	231.036
Radium	Ra	88	(226)
Radon	Rn	86	(222)
Rhenium	Re	75	186.207
Rhodium	Rh	45	102.9055
Roentgenium	Rg	111	(272)
Rubidium	Rb	37	85.4678
Ruthenium	Ru	44	101.07
Rutherfordium	Rf	104	(261)
Samarium	Sm	62	150.36
Scandium	Sc	21	44.9559
Seaborgium	Sg	106	(266)
Selenium	Se	34	78.96

ELEMENT	SYMBOL	ATOMIC NUMBER	ATOMIC MASS
Silicon	Si	14	28.0855
Silver	Ag	47	107.8682
Sodium	Na	11	22.9898
Strontium	Sr	38	87.62
Sulfur	S	16	32.067
Tantalum	Ta	73	180.948
Technetium	Tc	43	(98)
Tellurium	Te	52	127.6
Terbium	Tb	65	158.9253
Thallium	Tl	81	204.3833
Thorium	Th	90	232.0381
Thulium	Tm	69	168.9342
Tin	Sn	50	118.711
Titanium	Ti	22	47.867
Tungsten	W	74	183.84
Ununbium	Uub	112	(277)
Uranium	U	92	238.0289
Vanadium	V	23	50.9415
Xenon	Xe	54	131.29
Ytterbium	Yb	70	173.04
Yttrium	Y	39	88.906
Zinc	Zn	30	65.409
Zirconium	Zr	40	91.224

NOTES

1   American Institute of Physics, "A Look Inside the Atom," American Institute of Physics Web site. Available online. URL: http://aip.org/history/electron/jjhome.htm.

2   Barbara Lovett Cline, *Men Who Made a New Physics*. Chicago: University of Chicago Press, 1987, p. 107.

3   Ibid., p. 138.

4   Richard Rhodes, *The Making of the Atomic Bomb*. New York: Simon & Schuster, 1986, p. 162

5   Paul Strathern, *Mendeleyev's Dream: The Quest for the Elements*. New York: St. Martin's Press, 2001, p. 286.

6   James D. Watson (with Andrew Berry), *DNA: The Secret of Life*. New York: Alfred A. Knopf, 2003, p. 54.

7   Ranvet Veterinary Products, "Salt Licks." Available online. URL: http://www.ranvet.com.au/salt_licks.htm.

8   Arkansas Duck Hunter, "Salt Licks." Available online. URL: http://arkansasduckhunter.com/saltlick.asp.

GLOSSARY

Absolute temperature   The lowest possible temperature is absolute zero. The absolute temperature scale starts there and increases in increments of 1 degree Celsius. The unit of measurement is the kelvin (K).

Activation energy   The minimum energy required to start a chemical reaction.

Alkali metals   The very reactive metals found in Group 1 of the periodic table.

Alkaline earth metals   Those elements found in Group 2 of the periodic table.

Alpha particles   Helium nuclei composed of two protons and two neutrons that are emitted in radioactive decay.

Angular momentum   A measure of the intensity of rotational motion.

Angular momentum quantum number   This quantum number associated with the angular momentum of the electrons in an atom determines the shape of its orbitals.

Anode   The positively charged electrode in an electrolytic system.

Aromatic compound   Compounds derived from benzene.

Atoms   The smallest amount of an element that exhibits all of the element's properties.

Aufbau principle   The principle that states that the lowest-energy orbitals fill first when electrons are added to successive elements in the periodic table.

Base   A proton acceptor.

Beta particles   Energetic electrons emitted in radioactive decay.

Binding energy   A measure of the strength of the force holding the nucleons together in the nucleus of an atom. The term is sometimes applied to the force holding an electron in an atom.

Blackbody   A hypothetical body that absorbs all radiation that reaches it.

Brownian motion   The chaotic movement of microscopic particles suspended in a fluid.

Cathode   The negatively charged electrode in an electrolytic system.

Cathode rays   The stream of electrons emitted by the cathode in a vacuum tube.

Cathode ray tube   A tube with most of the air removed and two electrodes used to generate cathode rays.

Cation   A positively charged ion that migrates naturally to a cathode.

Chemical equilibrium   The state reached in a reversible reaction when the forward reaction is proceeding at the same rate as the reverse reaction.

Chemical reaction   The process that creates a chemical change.

Compound   A substance composed of two or more atoms joined by chemical bonds.

Covalent bonds   Bonds between atoms formed by sharing two or more valence electrons.

Dielectric constant   Also called *permittivity*. The dielectric constant of a substance is the ratio of the attractive force between two opposite charges measured in a vacuum to that force measured in the substance. The high dielectric constant of water makes it a good solvent for ionic compounds.

Diffraction grating   The most common gratings are made of reflecting or transparent sheets marked with fine parallel and equally spaced grooves or rulings. The grating separates polychromatic electromagnetic waves into their components. Similar results can be produced with a prism, but the mechanism is quite different. Fraunhofer used very fine parallel wires in his experiments.

Double bond   A covalent bond formed when four electrons are shared between two atoms.

Electric dipole   A molecule with two regions of opposite charge.

Electrolysis   The process for causing chemical change by passing a current between two electrodes. Cations, which are positively charged, will migrate to the cathode; anions to the anode.

Electromagnetic radiation   Massless energy waves that travel at 3.0×10^8 m sec^{-1} in a vacuum.

Electronegativity   A measure of the attracting power of an atom for an electron in a chemical bond.

Electron   A negatively charged particle found outside the nucleus of an atom. Free electrons are called beta particles.

Electron delocalization   Electrons in a molecule that are not associated with any particular bond or atom.

Element   A substance that cannot be split into simpler substances by chemical means.

Endothermic reaction   A chemical reaction that absorbs heat from its surroundings.

Enthalpy   A measure of the heat content of a substance or chemical system.

Entropy   A measure of randomness. Without the addition of energy, the entropy of a system tends to increase—to go from less random to more random.

Exothermic reaction   A chemical reaction that gives off heat.

Gamma rays   High-energy electromagnetic radiation. It is the most penetrating form of radiation that results from the decay of radioactive elements.

Gibbs free energy   A measure of a system's ability to do work. Changes in Gibbs free energy can be used to predict whether reactions will proceed spontaneously. In its most useful form, the equation for changes in Gibbs free energy is $\Delta G = \Delta H - T\Delta S$, where *G* is the Gibbs free energy, *H* is enthalpy, *T* is absolute temperature, and *S* is entropy.

Ground state   The lowest stable energy state of a system. The term is usually applied to atoms and molecules.

Half-life   The time it takes for half of any given amount of matter to undergo radioactive decay.

Halogens   The elements—fluorine, chlorine, bromine, iodine, and astatine—that make up Group 17 of the periodic table.

Heat of formation   The amount of heat absorbed or given off in forming one mole of a substance from its elements.

Hund's rule   Atoms in a higher total spin state are more stable than those in a lower spin state. When electrons are added to successive elements to form the periodic table, they fill different orbitals with electrons with the same spin before pairing up.

Hybridized orbital   The combination of atomic orbitals to form a new orbital.

Hydrogen bond   A weak bond between the hydrogen in a polar covalent bond and a neighboring molecule with a highly electronegative atom.

Hydrophilic   Water-loving.

Integer   A positive or negative whole number.

Interference pattern   The pattern generated when two or more waves interact with one another.

Ion   An atom that carries an electric charge due to the addition or removal of one or more electrons.

Ionic bond   The bond between ions due to their opposite electrical charges.

Ionization energy   The energy required to remove an electron from an atom or ion in the gaseous state.

Isotopes   Atoms with the same number of protons and electrons but with a different number of neutrons in the nucleus. Isotopes of an element act the same chemically but differ in mass.

Joule   The SI unit of work. Abbreviated J, it is equal to 0.2388 calories.

Kinetic energy   The energy of motion. The classical equation for kinetic energy of a body is $mv^2/2$, where m is the mass of the body and v is its velocity.

Magnetic quantum number   One solution to Schrödinger's wave equation produces the magnetic quantum number. It specifies how the s, p, d, and f orbitals are oriented in space.

Mass   A measure of the quantity of matter. On Earth, weight is used to indicate the mass of an object.

Matter   Anything with an at-rest mass greater than zero.

Metallic bonding   The bonding present in metallic crystals composed of a lattice of positively charged atoms in a sea of delocalized electrons.

Miscible   A term used to specify the degree that two substances will mix with one another. Completely miscible substances such as water and ethanol will mix uniformly no matter the proportions.

Molar solution   A solution containing 1 mole of solute in 1 liter of solution.

Mole   A measure of the number of particles. One mole contains 6.02×10^{23} particles.

Molecular formula   A formula such as H_2O that shows the number of and type of atoms in a molecule.

Molecular orbital   The orbitals for electrons in a molecule. Molecular orbitals are calculated by combining the wave functions of the highest-energy orbitals of the atoms in the molecule.

Molecules   Molecules are made from atoms joined by chemical bonds. They are the smallest part of a substance that retains all the properties of that substance.

Momentum   Momentum is the force of motion of a moving body. Quantitatively, it is the product of its mass of the object multiplied by its velocity, $p = mv$.

Monochromatic light   Electromagnetic radiation of a single wavelength in the visible range.

Neutron   A subatomic particle found in the nuclei of atoms. It is electrically neutral with a mass that is slightly greater than that of a proton.

Nucleon   A proton or neutron.

Orbital   A subdivision of an energy shell where there is a high probability of finding an electron. An orbital can contain a maximum of two electrons.

Organic molecules   Molecules that contain one or more atoms of carbon.

Pauli exclusion principle   No two electrons in an atom can possess an identical set of quantum numbers.

Periodic table   A chart that arranges the elements by atomic number in a way that the vertical columns produce groups of elements with similar valence electron configurations and chemical properties.

Phosphorescent   The ability of a substance to emit light and to continue to glow after the exciting source of energy has been removed.

Photoelectric effect   The effect produced when electromagnetic radiation knocks electrons out of a metal. Einstein used this phenomenon to show that light was quantized and came in energy packets called photons.

Photon   A particle with energy but no at-rest mass. It represents a quantum of electromagnetic radiation.

Polar covalent bond   A bond between atoms of different electronegativities in which the electrons are closer to one atom than the other. This leaves a slight positive charge on one atom in the molecule and a slight negative charge on the other.

Positron   The antiparticle of an electron. It is a particle with mass of an electron but with a positive electric charge of the same magnitude as the electron's negative charge.

Positron emission tomography (PET)   A medical imaging technique that helps physicians locate tumors and other growths in the body. A radioactive tracer isotope which emits a positron is incorporated into a metabolically active molecule. A scanner locates the tissues where the radioactive substance winds up.

Principal quantum number   This quantum number specifies the main energy shells of an atom. It corresponds roughly to the distance between the nucleus and the orbital. Its symbol is n.

Proton   The positively charged subatomic particle found in the nucleus of atoms.

Quanta   The plural of quantum. It is the minimum energy required to change certain properties such as the energy of an electron in an atom.

Quantum numbers   The four quantum numbers—principal, angular momentum, magnetic, and spin—arise from solutions to the wave equation and govern the electron configuration of atoms.

Radioactive decay   A process in which an element emits radiation, creating a new element.

Radioactive elements   Elements capable of emitting alpha, beta, or gamma radiation.

Resonance   Molecules with two or more valid structures are said to be resonant. The actual structure is neither of the alternatives but a lower-energy molecule with delocalized valence electrons. Benzene with its alternating double and single bonds is an example of a resonant structure. Benzene actually has no single or double bonds. Its real structure lies somewhere between the two possibilities.

Reversible reaction   A reaction that can go forward or backward. Its end point is an equilibrium between reactants and reaction products.

Salt lick   Aboveground salt deposits used by deer, buffalo, and other animals to get the supplemental salt they need.

Scientific notation   A method for expressing numbers in the form of exponents of 10, such as $10^2 = 100$, $10^3 = 1,000$, and $6,020 = 6.02 \times 10^3$.

Scintillation   The flash of light emitted when an electron in an excited state drops to a lower energy level. Scintillation counters are designed to measure the intensity of emissions from radioactive materials.

Spectroscopy   The science of analyzing the spectra of atoms and molecules. Emission spectroscopy deals with exciting atoms or molecules and measuring the wavelength of the emitted electromagnetic radiation. Absorption spectroscopy measures the wavelengths of absorbed radiation.

Spontaneous reaction   A reaction where the Gibbs free energy is negative. Such reactions proceed naturally without requiring added energy after initiation.

Strong force   The force that holds the atomic nucleus together. It operates only at very short distances.

Structural formula   A formula that illustrates the arrangement of the atoms in a molecule. H-O-H, for example.

Surface tension   The attraction between molecules that tends to pull the molecules at the surface of a liquid down. This makes the surface become as small as possible and makes certain substances—water, for instance—act as though a thin membrane was stretched across the surface.

TNT The abbreviation for trinitrotoluene. It is a much more stable compound than nitroglycerine but still capable of producing a powerful explosion when detonated.

Transition elements Elements in Groups 3 through 12 in the periodic table. These elements have partially filled d orbitals, but the number of valence electrons varies. Consequently, they have widely different chemical properties.

Transmutation The conversion of one element into another by natural radioactive decay or by bombarding it with radiation.

Triple bond A covalent bond formed when six electrons are shared between two atoms.

Uncertainty principle The principle developed by Werner Heisenberg that it is not possible to know the momentum and position of a particle with unlimited accuracy.

Valence The highest-energy electrons in an atom, which an atom loses, gains, or shares in forming a chemical bond.

Valence shell electron-pair repulsion (VSEPR) A procedure based on electron repulsion in molecules that enables chemists to predict approximate bond angles.

X-rays High-energy electromagnetic radiation usually produced by the action of high-energy electrons hitting a solid target.

BIBLIOGRAPHY

American Institute of Physics. "A Look Inside the Atom." Available online. URL: http://aip.org/history/electron/jjhome.htm.

Campbell, John. "Rutherford: A Brief Biography." Available online. URL: http://www.rutherford.org.nz/biography.htm.

City University of New York. "The Discovery of Protons." Available online. URL: http://www.brooklyn.cuny.edu/bc/ahp/LAD/C3/C3_Protons.html.

Clackamas Community College. "Atomic Size." Available online. URL: http://dl.clackamas.cc.or.us/ch104-07/atomic_size.htm.

Cline, Barbara Lovett. *Men Who Made a New Physics.* Chicago: University of Chicago Press, 1987.

Egglescliffe School. "Black Body Radiation." Available online. URL: http://www.egglescliffe.org.uk/physics/astronomy/blackbody/bbody.html.

Emsley, John. *Nature's Building Blocks: An A–Z Guide to the Elements.* New York: Oxford University Press, 2001.

Feynman, Richard P. *Six Easy Pieces: Essentials of Physics Explained by Its Most Brilliant Teacher.* Cambridge, Mass.: Helix Books, 1963.

Florida State University. "Electron Configurations and the Periodic Table." Available online. URL: http://wine1.sb.fsu.edu/chm1045/notes/Struct/EPeriod/Struct09.htm.

Georgia State University. "Nuclear Binding Energy." Available online. URL: http://hyperphysics.phy-astr.gsu.edu/hbase/nucene/nucbin.html.

Georgia State University. "Physical Properties of Some Typical Liquids." Available online. URL: http://hyperphysics.phy-astr.gsu.edu/hbase/tables/liqprop.html.

Gray, Harry B. *Chemical Bonds: An Introduction to Atomic and Molecular Structure.* Menlo Park, Calif.: W.A. Benjamin, Inc., 1973.

Greenaway, Frank. *John Dalton and the Atom*. Ithaca, N.Y.: Cornell University Press, 1966.

Gribbin, John. *In Search of Schrödinger's Cat: Quantum Physics and Reality*. New York: Bantam Books, 1984.

Imperial College. "Introduction to Molecular Orbital Theory." Available online. URL: http://www.ch.ic.ac.uk/vchemlib/ course/mo_theory/main.html.

International Union of Pure and Applied Chemistry (IUPAC). "IUPAC Periodic Table of the Elements." Available online. URL: http://www.iupac.org/reports/periodic_table/IUPAC_ Periodic_Table-3Oct05.pdf.

Kennesaw State University. "Nuclear Chemistry: Discovery of the Neutron (1932)." Available online. URL: http://www. chemcases.com/nuclear/nc-01.htm.

Kurlansky, Mark. *Salt: A World History*. New York: Walker and Company, 2002.

Lide, David R., ed. *CRC Handbook of Chemistry and Physics*. 79th ed. New York: CRC Press, 1998.

Mascetta, Joseph A. *Chemistry the Easy Way*. Hauppage, N.Y.: Barrons, 2003.

Moeller, Therald. *Inorganic Chemistry: An Advanced Textbook*. New York: John Wiley & Sons, 1952.

Moore, John T. *Chemistry for Dummies*. Hoboken, N.J.: Wiley Publishing, Inc., 2003.

Ne'eman, Yuval and Yoram Kirsh. *The Particle Hunters*. Cambridge, England: Cambridge University Press, 1996.

New York University. "Water and Ice." Available online. URL: http://www.nyu.edu/pages/mathmol/textbook/info_water. html.

Pais, Abraham. *Inward Bound: Of Matter and Forces in the Physical World*. New York: Oxford University Press, 1986.

Parker, Barry. *Einstein: The Passions of a Scientist*. Amherst, N.Y.: Prometheus Books, 2003.

Purdue University. "The Activation Energy of Chemical Reactions." Available online. URL: http://chemed.chem.purdue.edu/genchem/topicreview/bp/ch22/activate.html.

Rhodes, Richard. *The Making of the Atomic Bomb*. New York: Simon & Schuster, 1986.

Rozental, S., ed. *Niels Bohr: His Life and Work as Seen by His Friends and Colleagues*. Amsterdam: North-Holland Publishing Co., 1967.

ScienceGeek.net. "Los Alamos National Laboratory Chemistry Division, Periodic Table of the Elements." Available online. URL: http://www.sciencegeek.net/tables/LosAlamosperiodictableColor.pdf.

Shodor Education Foundation. "Chem Viz: Background Reading for Ionization Energy." Available online. URL: http://www.shodor.org/chemviz/ionization/students/background.html.

Strathern, Paul. *Mendeleyev's Dream: The Quest for the Elements*. New York: St. Martin's Press, 2001.

University of Minnesota-Morris. "Water & Hydrogen Bonding." Available online. URL: http://chemed.chem.purdue.edu/genchem/topicreview/bp/ch22/activate.html.

Walter, Alan E. *Radiation and Modern Life: Fulfilling Madame Curie's Dream*. Amherst, N.Y.: Prometheus Books, 2004.

Watson, James D. (with Andrew Berry). *DNA: The Secret of Life*. New York: Alfred A. Knopf, 2003.

Wilbraham, Anthony C., Dennis D. Staley, Michael S. Matta, and Edward L. Waterman. *Chemistry*. Boston: Prentice Hall, Inc., 2005.

FURTHER READING

Cathcart, Brian. *The Fly in the Cathedral: How a Group of Cambridge Scientists Won the International Race to Split the Atom.* New York: Farrar, Straus, and Giroux, 2004.

Cline, Barbara Lovett. *Men Who Made a New Physics.* Chicago: University of Chicago Press, 1987.

LeCouteur, Penny and Jay Burreson. *Napoleon's Buttons: How 17 Molecules Changed History.* New York: Jeremy P. Tarcher/Putnam, 2003.

Levi, Primo. *The Periodic Table.* New York: Schocken Books, 1984.

Rhodes, Richard. *The Making of the Atomic Bomb.* New York: Simon & Schuster, 1986.

Sacks, Oliver. *Uncle Tungsten: Memories of a Chemical Boyhood.* New York: Alfred A. Knopf, 2001.

Walker, Stephen. *Shockwave: Countdown to Hiroshima.* New York: Harper Collins, 2005.

Watson, James D. *The Double Helix.* New York: Atheneum, 1968.

Web Sites

The Discovery of the Electron
http://aip.org/history/electron/

Interactive Periodic Table of the Elements
http://www.chemicalelements.com

The Orbitron: A Gallery of Atomic Orbitals and Molecular Orbitals
http://winter.group.shef.ac.uk/orbitron/

Rutherford: A Brief Biography
http://www.rutherford.org.nz/biography.htm

Thomas Young's Double Slit Experiment
http://micro.magnet.fsu.edu/primer/java/interference/doubleslit

A Visual Interpretation of the Table of Elements
http://www.chemsoc.org/VISELEMENTS/

PHOTO CREDITS

All illustrations © Infobase Publishing.
Cover photograph © Max Planck Institute for Metallurgy/Photo Researchers, Inc.

INDEX

ABOUT THE AUTHOR

PHILLIP MANNING is the author of four other books and 150 or so magazine and newspaper articles. His most recent book, *Islands of Hope*, won the 1999 National Outdoor Book Award for nature and the environment. Manning has a Ph.D. in physical chemistry from the University of North Carolina at Chapel Hill. His Web site (www.scibooks.org) offers a weekly list of new books of science and science book reviews.

Manning was assisted in this project by Dr. Richard C. Jarnagin, who taught chemistry at the University of North Carolina for many years. He mentored numerous graduate students, including the author. In assisting with this book, he caught many errors. Those that remain, however, are the sole responsibility of the author.